Maya Grace

The Magic of Manifestation
Unlocking Your Unlimited Potential

Original Title: A Magia da Manifestação - Desbloqueando o seu Potencial Ilimitado.

Copyright © 2025, published by Luiz Antonio dos Santos ME.

This book is a non-fiction work exploring practices and concepts in the field of personal development and manifestation. Through a comprehensive approach, the author provides practical tools to achieve emotional balance, prosperity, and personal fulfillment.

1st Edition
Production Team
Author: Maya Grace
Editor: Luiz Santos
Cover Design: Studios Booklas
Typesetting: Jonathan Reeves
Translation: Emily Harper
Consultants & Researchers: Dr. Michael Lawson, Sophia Bennett, Daniel Carter

Publication and Identification
The Magic of Manifestation
Booklas Publishing, 2025
Categories: Personal Development / Spirituality / Consciousness Studies
DDC: 158.1 - **CDU:** 159.923.2

All rights reserved to:

Luiz Antonio dos Santos ME / Booklas Publishing No part of this book may be reproduced, stored in a retrieval system, or transmitted by any means—electronic, mechanical, photocopying, recording, or otherwise—without prior and express authorization from the copyright holder.

Sumário

Sistematic Index 5
Prologue 11
Chapter 1 The Cosmic Mirror 13
Chapter 2 The Dream We Call Reality 20
Chapter 3 The Nature of the One Consciousness (God) 25
Chapter 4 Fragments of Divinity 30
Chapter 5 Conceptual Knowledge 36
Chapter 6 Thoughts, Beliefs, and Reality 42
Chapter 7 Shared Reality 47
Chapter 8 Recognizing Your Power 53
Chapter 9 The First Step 59
Chapter 10 Releasing Limiting Beliefs 65
Chapter 11 Focusing Your Intentions and Desires 72
Chapter 12 The Power of Visualization 80
Chapter 13 Declaring Your New Reality 88
Chapter 14 Attracting Abundance and Joy 96
Chapter 15 Amplifying Your Projection 103
Chapter 16 Overcoming Resistance 110
Chapter 17 Flowing with the Universe and Releasing Control 117
Chapter 18 Conscious Co-creation in Motion 125
Chapter 19 Co-creating Relationships 133
Chapter 20 Projecting Fulfillment and Contribution 141
Chapter 21 Living a Projected Reality 148
Chapter 22 Co-creating Health 156
Chapter 23 Co-creating Abundance 164

Chapter 24 Learning to Project Peace 173
Chapter 25 Co-creating Travels 182
Chapter 26 Unlocking Creative Potential 191
Chapter 27 Co-creating the Manifestation of Dreams 200
Chapter 28 Co-creating Beyond the Individual 210
Chapter 29 Habits and Continuous Practices............................ 218
Chapter 30 Expansion and New Horizons 227

Sistematic Index

Chapter 1: The Cosmic Mirror - Introduces the concept of conscious projection, where reality is seen as a reflection of the One Consciousness, and explores the motivation behind this projection.

Chapter 2: The Dream We Call Reality - Explores the analogy of reality as a collective dream, drawing parallels with spiritual traditions and quantum physics, and discusses the implications of this perspective for our lives.

Chapter 3: The Nature of the One Consciousness (God) - Delves into the attributes of the One Consciousness, emphasizing its omnipresence, omnipotence, and omniscience, and clarifies misconceptions about its nature, advocating for a view free of limiting beliefs.

Chapter 4: Fragments of Divinity - Presents the concept of human beings as inseparable fragments of the One Consciousness, endowed with free will and co-creative power, and discusses the purpose of human existence within this framework.

Chapter 5: Conceptual Knowledge - Differentiates between conceptual knowledge and experiential living, explaining the One Consciousness's motivation for projection as a means of transforming knowledge into direct experience and exploring the totality of existence.

Chapter 6: Thoughts, Beliefs, and Reality - Explains how thoughts and beliefs actively shape reality, acting as a "code" that directs the projection of our experiences, and emphasizes the importance of conscious management of our mental landscape for co-creation.

Chapter 7: Shared Reality - Introduces the concept of Shared Reality, shaped by the Collective Consciousness, and explores how collective beliefs and paradigms influence individual experiences, while also highlighting the potential for individual awakening to transform Shared Reality.

Chapter 8: Recognizing Your Power - Emphasizes the shift from theory to practical action, urging readers to recognize their innate co-creative power and take responsibility for their reality, marking a turning point in the book towards active co-creation.

Chapter 9: The First Step - Highlights the importance of self-awareness and observation of thoughts as the foundation for conscious co-creation, providing practical techniques and exercises to cultivate mindfulness and mental "etiquette."

Chapter 10: Releasing Limiting Beliefs - Guides readers through the process of identifying, dismantling, and replacing limiting beliefs with empowering ones, using techniques such as logical questioning, reframing experiences, and positive affirmations.

Chapter 11: Focusing Your Intentions and Desires - Explains the importance of setting clear, specific, and authentic intentions aligned with personal values and purpose, using affirmative language and combining intention with visualization and emotion for powerful manifestation.

Chapter 12: The Power of Visualization - Presents visualization as a powerful tool for co-creation, explaining how it influences the subconscious mind and aligns emotions with the desired reality, providing detailed instructions and exercises for effective visualization practice.

Chapter 13: Declaring Your New Reality - Introduces affirmations as a way to reprogram the subconscious mind and direct energy towards manifestation, providing detailed guidelines on formulating and practicing affirmations effectively, along with examples for various areas of life.

Chapter 14: Attracting Abundance and Joy - Focuses on gratitude as a key to unlocking abundance and joy, explaining its transformative effects on our energy and perception, and offering practical techniques to cultivate gratitude in daily life.

Chapter 15: Amplifying Your Projection - Explores how positive emotions amplify manifestation by raising our vibrational frequency and strengthening belief, offering practical strategies to cultivate and integrate positive emotions into the co-creation process.

Chapter 16: Overcoming Resistance - Addresses the internal and external challenges that arise in co-creation, providing strategies to overcome resistance, reframe challenges, and navigate obstacles with awareness, patience, and self-compassion.

Chapter 17: Flowing with the Universe and Releasing Control - Emphasizes the balance between intention and surrender, explaining how releasing the need for control and trusting the universe can lead to more harmonious and expansive manifestations.

Chapter 18: Conscious Co-creation in Motion - Explains how inspired action bridges intention and manifestation, discussing the characteristics of inspired action and providing strategies to integrate it into daily life, aligning actions with intuition and purpose.

Chapter 19: Co-creating Relationships - Applies the principles of co-creation to relationships, emphasizing the mirror effect and offering guidance on how to co-create harmonious relationships through unconditional love, empathy, clear communication, and forgiveness.

Chapter 20: Projecting Fulfillment and Contribution - Explores the co-creation of life purpose and career, offering principles and practices to align professional and personal life with one's authentic self, leading to a fulfilling and meaningful contribution to the world.

Chapter 21: Living a Projected Reality - Integrates the principles and practices of co-creation into a holistic lifestyle, guiding readers to embody co-creation in all areas of life, transforming daily experiences into conscious manifestations of intention.

Chapter 22: Co-creating Health - Discusses health as a natural state of balance and explains how co-creation principles can be applied to achieve radiant health and well-being, offering guidance on conscious nutrition, movement, rest, and connection with nature.

Chapter 23: Co-creating Abundance - Explores the concept of abundance as the natural state of the universe and provides guidance on how to co-create financial abundance and prosperity by transforming limiting beliefs, visualizing wealth, and practicing gratitude.

Chapter 24: Learning to Project Peace - Focuses on co-creating a harmonious home and sacred space as an extension of inner peace, offering principles and practices to transform living spaces into sanctuaries of tranquility and well-being.

Chapter 25: Co-creating Travels - Explores travel as a soul journey and offers guidance on how to co-create magical travel experiences through intention, visualization, affirmations, and openness to synchronicity and cultural immersion.

Chapter 26: Unlocking Creative Potential - Discusses creativity as an innate human ability and explains how to co-create creative solutions and innovation by setting clear intentions, visualizing creative outcomes, and cultivating positive emotions.

Chapter 27: Co-creating the Manifestation of Dreams - Provides advanced principles and techniques for manifesting specific dreams, including detailed visualization, personalized affirmations, creative scripting, and emotional release techniques.

Chapter 28: Co-creating Beyond the Individual - Emphasizes the power of collective co-creation for the greater good, offering principles and strategies for aligning intentions, cultivating harmony in groups, and taking inspired collective action.

Chapter 29: Habits and Continuous Practices - Guides readers on how to maintain conscious co-creation as a lifelong practice through daily habits, continuous learning, and connection with a community of co-creators.

Chapter 30: Expansion and New Horizons - Concludes the book by emphasizing the ongoing nature of the co-creation journey, encouraging readers to embrace expansion, explore new possibilities, and continue their conscious dance with the universe.

Prologue

There are books that inform. There are books that entertain. And there are books that awaken. This is one of them.

If you have found *The Magic of Manifestation*, it is not by chance. There is a silent call that leads us exactly to the knowledge we need at the right time. And maybe, now, it is your turn to awaken to a reality where you are not just a spectator, but the architect of your own existence.

What you will find here are not mere theories about positive thinking or superficial recipes to attract good things. No. This book is a map to access something that has always been within you: your unlimited potential.

We live surrounded by beliefs that make us feel powerless, that make us believe that we are at the mercy of circumstances, chance, and external limitations. But what if I told you that all this is just a projection? What if the reality around you was actually a reflection of your own consciousness? And what if you could reprogram that projection to manifest health, abundance, love, and purpose?

This book brings answers. But more than that, it offers tools. With each page, you will learn to identify the hidden patterns that shape your life, dissolve limiting beliefs, and design a reality aligned with your most authentic desires. You will discover that manifestation is not an esoteric whim - it is a skill that can be mastered, a conscious dance with the universe, where your thoughts, emotions, and intentions become the brushes that paint your existence.

But beware: this reading is not for those seeking easy shortcuts or instant miracles. This book is a call for those who are ready to take their own lives into their hands and understand, once and for all, that manifesting is not wishing - it is knowing how to consciously co-create with the universe.

If you feel a shiver as you read these words, a restlessness or an enthusiasm that you cannot explain, follow that sign. *The Magic of Manifestation* has something to reveal to you.

Now, the choice is yours: to continue seeing life as a random sequence of events or to awaken to your true power.

The journey begins on the next page. Are you ready?

Chapter 1
The Cosmic Mirror

Imagine yourself standing in front of a colossal mirror, a mirror that not only reflects your image, but that contains within itself the vastness of the universe, the complexity of life, and the myriad of experiences that make up the tapestry of existence. This mirror, in fact, is not made of glass or metal, but of the very essence of consciousness. This is the starting point of our journey: the hypothesis of conscious projection, the radical and transformative idea that everything, absolutely everything we perceive and experience, is a projection emanating from a single source of consciousness.

This is not one theory among many, nor a passing belief. For the purposes of this book, and for the profound transformation it aims to awaken in you, we will embrace this hypothesis as an absolute truth, a fundamental principle upon which we can build a new understanding of reality and, more importantly, a new way of interacting with it.

Let's call this single source of consciousness "Unique Consciousness" or, to facilitate familiarity and without dogmatic religious pretensions, we can even use the name "God." It is crucial, from the beginning, to strip this term of any limiting connotations or prejudices that you may have acquired throughout your life. Here, "God" does not represent an anthropomorphic, judgmental, or distant figure, but rather the very creative, omnipresent, and omnipotent essence from which everything emanates. It is the fundamental matrix, the infinite ocean of potentiality from which arises the projection of the reality we know.

The Unique Consciousness, in this context, holds a conceptual knowledge of everything there is to know. Imagine the largest library in the universe, containing every book, every formula, every work of art, every possible experience, cataloged and accessible. The Unique Consciousness possesses this knowledge in its entirety, in a conceptual, comprehensive, and perfect way. However, having the map is not the same as walking the territory. Knowing the recipe for a cake is not the same as tasting it fresh from the oven. This is where the primary motivation for projection lies.

To make this concept more tangible, let's use a simple and impactful analogy: imagine yourself on the edge of a frozen lake. You know, conceptually, what happens when you jump into icy water. You know the effects: the thermal shock, the sharp sensation of cold, the possible numbness, the gasping for breath. You can read about it, watch movies, hear accounts from others. But this knowledge remains conceptual, distant, mere intellectual information. The reality of the experience, the visceral impact of the cold, the response of your body and mind, is only revealed when you actually jump into the icy water and feel for yourself what you previously only knew in theory.

In the same way, the Unique Consciousness, possessing all conceptual knowledge, yearns for experiential living. It wants to feel, taste, explore, and understand the myriad of possibilities that reside in its infinite potential. And what way does it find to fulfill this desire? Projection.

The Unique Consciousness projects itself in myriads of forms, dividing itself, apparently, into everything that exists. Every star in the night sky, every grain of sand on the beach, every leaf that sways in the wind, every human being who walks on Earth - everything, without exception, is a manifestation, a projection of this Unique Consciousness. It is as if a single ray of light were fragmented as it passed through a prism, giving rise to a spectrum of vibrant colors. Although the colors appear distinct and separate, they are all, ultimately, manifestations of the same original light.

Thus, everything we see and experience, all the complexity and beauty of the world around us, is nothing more than the projection of this Unique Consciousness experiencing itself. You, as a reader, I as a writer, the air we breathe, the ground we walk on, the emotions we feel, the thoughts that cross our minds - we are all fragments, projections, extensions of this Unique Consciousness, each playing a unique and essential role in the great dance of experience.

The exact dimension where the Unique Consciousness exists, the nature of its primordial reality, transcends our capacity for linear and logical understanding, limited as we are by our three-dimensional experience and our perception conditioned by projection. It is like trying to describe the ocean to a fish that has always lived in it, or explaining the experience of color to someone who was born blind. The tools of our conceptual mind and our language fail when trying to capture the essence of this transcendent dimension. It simply "is," a field of pure potentiality, the ineffable source of all manifestation.

In this hypothesis, the Unique Consciousness is simultaneously the subject and object of all experience. It is the person who feels hungry and also the food that satisfies that hunger. It is the killer and the victim, in an apparent paradox that dissolves when we understand the illusory nature of separation in projection. It is the cause and effect, the beginning and the end, the alpha and omega of all that exists. Absolutely everything, ultimately, returns to this Unique Consciousness, like rivers that flow into the ocean, like rays of light that return to their primordial source.

And where do we, human beings, fit into this vast cosmic panorama? In this hypothesis, each human being is a unique and precious fragment of this Unique Consciousness, a particular facet of its self-experience. Our individual existence, with all its joys and sorrows, successes and failures, loves and losses, is like a singular dream, rich in detail and emotions, but which inevitably comes to an end. At the moment of death, when the physical body ceases its functions, this individual fragment of consciousness, which we call a "human being," returns to the whole, merging again with the Unique Consciousness, bringing with it the unique baggage of experiences and wisdom accumulated during its journey in the projection.

It is important to emphasize that this "return" does not imply the loss of individuality or the extinction of consciousness. On the contrary, it is a reintegration, an enrichment of the whole with the unique and irreplaceable essence of each fragment. Imagine an infinite cosmic puzzle, where each piece, representing a human life, fits into the perfect place, contributing to the beauty and complexity of the total image.

In this format, everything we know, everything we perceive as reality, is fundamentally a projection, a construction of consciousness. And as a projection, reality becomes malleable, influenceable, responding to our thoughts, beliefs, and intentions. Just as in a lucid dream, where the dreamer becomes aware of the dreamlike nature of the dream and begins to shape it according to their will, so too in the "projected reality" we have the potential to influence and even materialize our desires, simply by focusing on what we truly want.

This is the bold and liberating promise of the conscious projection hypothesis: the power to co-create our reality, to become conscious artists on the canvas of existence. But if everything is projection, if we have this inherent power, why then are we not all healthy, wealthy, and able to fly like birds, simply by wishing it? This is the inevitable question, the objection that naturally arises in the mind.

The answer lies in the understanding that we are not unique and isolated projections, but rather interconnected fragments of the same Unique Consciousness. We all, collectively, participate in the projection of reality. And collective beliefs, shared expectations, the dominant paradigms of collective consciousness exert a powerful influence on what manifests in our individual and collective experience.

If the dominant belief is that disease, poverty, and limitations are inevitable, if the collective consciousness projects the idea that "you cannot have health," "you cannot be rich," "you cannot fly," then the Unique Consciousness, encompassing all individual consciousnesses, manifests this projected reality on a large scale. It is like an unconscious consensus, a collective programming that is self-reinforcing.

That is why changing reality is not an instant magical act, a mere "wish and receive." It takes an awakening of consciousness, a gradual transformation of beliefs and thought patterns, both individually and collectively. It is necessary to "activate the mind," as mentioned in your premise, and begin to "make small changes," gradually, consistently, until the practice of mastering conscious projection becomes a natural and powerful skill.

And so, understanding the projected nature of reality is not just a philosophical exercise, but an invitation to conscious transformation. If we are fragments of this Unique Consciousness, then we have within us the same creative spark capable of shaping experience. The key to this change is not to deny the collective projection, but to learn to navigate through it, to recognize patterns, dissolve limitations, and expand the perception of the possible. Each adjusted thought, each belief reformulated, each intention aligned with this greater understanding brings us closer to mastering conscious projection. And it is on this path that we now embark: a journey to awaken, recognize, and claim our true nature as co-creators of existence.

Chapter 2
The Dream We Call Reality

Think for a moment about the experience of a dream. When you are dreaming, the world around you seems as real, as concrete, as tangible as the world you experience when you are awake. In the dream, you interact with people, places and objects that seem to have their own existence. You feel intense emotions, joys, fears, sorrows. You can run, fly, fall, love, fight – the range of possible experiences is vast and often indistinguishable from "waking" reality.

However, upon waking, the illusion fades. You realize that the dream world, with all its sensory and emotional richness, was nothing more than a construct of your own mind. The people, the places, the objects, the situations – everything was, ultimately, an internal projection, a dance of images and sensations created by your own consciousness. The dream, however vivid and engaging it may have been, is revealed as something ephemeral, insubstantial, a parallel reality that dissolves as the fog of sleep dissipates.

Now, I invite you to contemplate a fundamental question: what if the reality we experience in the waking state, the reality we call "reality", shared, in essence, the same dreamlike nature? What if the world around us, with all its apparent solidity and permanence, were also, ultimately, a projection, a collective "dream" of the One Consciousness, of which we are participants and co-creators?

This is not a new or eccentric idea. Throughout history, in various cultures and spiritual traditions, we find echoes of this perspective. The Hindu Vedas speak of "Maya", the cosmic illusion that veils the true nature of reality. Buddhism emphasizes the empty and impermanent nature of all phenomena, comparing reality to a dream or a mirage. In Western philosophy, thinkers like Plato, with his allegory of the cave, and more recently philosophers and quantum physicists, have questioned the fundamental nature of material reality, pointing to the possibility that the world we perceive is more "mind-like" than "matter-like".

The conscious projection hypothesis radicalizes this line of thought, proposing that all of existence is, in fact, a projection of the One Consciousness. And to better understand this idea, we can resort to other metaphors and analogies that help us to "feel" the illusory nature of solid material reality.

Think, for example, of a holographic projection. A hologram creates a seemingly solid three-dimensional image that appears to float in space. We can even try to touch the hologram, but we realize that there is nothing there, just light and interference patterns. The holographic image is a perceptual illusion, a projection of information that creates the appearance of solidity and three-dimensionality where, in fact, only energy and information exist.

In the same way, the reality we perceive can be compared to a cosmic hologram, a projection of the One Consciousness that creates the illusion of a solid, separate and independent material world. Quantum physics, with its surprising discoveries about the nature of matter and energy, has been corroborating this view. At the subatomic level, matter is revealed not as solid particles, but as probabilities, waves of vibrant energy, information in constant flux. The solidity that we perceive in the macroscopic world emerges, according to this perspective, from our interaction with quantum reality, from our observation and consciousness.

Another useful metaphor is that of film or video game. In a film, we see characters, scenarios, actions unfolding on a screen. We get emotionally involved with the story, identify with the characters, experience their adventures and misadventures. But we know, deep down, that all of that is not "real" in the conventional sense. It is a sequence of projected images, an illusion of movement and life created by the projection of frames at high speed.

In the same way, our daily reality can be seen as a "cosmic film" or a "consciousness video game", where we are simultaneously the players and the avatars, the observers and the participants in the narrative. The One Consciousness, the ultimate "director" or "programmer", projects the experience, and we, as conscious fragments of this Consciousness, immerse ourselves in the illusion, experiencing the emotions, challenges and opportunities that the projected reality presents us.

It is crucial to understand that this dreamlike or illusory nature of reality does not imply that the experience is less valid or meaningful. A dream can be incredibly real and impactful while we are experiencing it, even knowing that, upon waking, it will dissipate. In the same way, our individual existence, even if understood as a "dream within the Greater Dream of the One Consciousness", is deeply valuable, rich in learning and opportunities for growth and evolution.

The ephemerality of individual existence, the fact that our human journey has a beginning and an end, is not a reason for despair or nihilism, but rather an invitation to fully appreciate the present moment, to value each experience, each relationship, each instant of consciousness. Just like a beautiful dream that we know will end at dawn, our life becomes even more precious and meaningful when we understand its transitory nature.

Understanding the dreamlike nature of reality also frees us from excessive attachment to form and matter. If everything is projection, then the solidity, permanence and separation that we perceive in the material world are ultimately illusions. The true essence of reality lies in the One Consciousness, in the primordial source of projection, which is eternal, infinite and unchanging.

This knowledge can bring a profound sense of peace and freedom. We free ourselves from the fear of death, the anxiety of loss and the illusion of separation. We understand that, ultimately, we are all part of the same One Consciousness, interconnected and interdependent, dancing together in the same "cosmic dream".

Throughout this book, we will explore the practical implications of this understanding of the dreamlike nature of reality for our daily lives. How can this perspective transform the way we face challenges, relationships, our health, our prosperity and our life purpose? How can we use this knowledge to become conscious co-creators of our reality, shaping the "dream" according to our most authentic and highest desires?

The answer to these questions lies not only in theory, but in the practice of awakened consciousness. If reality is a collective dream, then the key to transforming our experience lies in lucidity within that dream. Just as a lucid dreamer realizes that he is dreaming and begins to interact with the dream consciously, we too can learn to recognize the illusory patterns of our existence and shape them with intention and clarity. Each thought aligned with this understanding becomes a thread that weaves a new narrative, a new possibility within the projection. The question that arises, then, is not only whether we are dreaming, but how we want to dream from now on.

Chapter 3
The Nature of the One Consciousness (God)

Manifest reality is the direct expression of the One Consciousness, the fundamental matrix of all existence. It is not an abstract or distant concept, but the very substance of all that is, the primordial source that sustains and permeates every aspect of the universe. To understand this essence, it is necessary to free oneself from limited conceptions that restrict it to a separate or anthropomorphic entity. The One Consciousness is not a being with human attributes, but an infinite field of potentiality, absolute cosmic intelligence, omnipresent and omnipotent, whose nature transcends any definition.

The One Consciousness, the "Architect of All", is not a personal entity in the human sense, with a physical body, an audible voice or an individualized ego. It transcends the limitations of form and definition, existing on a level of reality that surpasses our linear and three-dimensional understanding. It is best understood as an infinite field of pure potentiality, an omnipresent and omnipotent cosmic intelligence, the very essence of creation and existence.

Let's explore some of the fundamental attributes of this One Consciousness, recognizing that any verbal or conceptual description will always be a pale approximation of its true magnitude and mystery.

Firstly, the One Consciousness is Omnipresent. This means that it is present everywhere, at all times, in all things. There is not a single point in space or time, manifest or unmanifest, where the One Consciousness is not present. It permeates everything, penetrates everything, sustains everything. It is the very basis of existence, the fundamental substrate upon which the projection of reality manifests. Imagine the ocean, vast and boundless, containing within itself all the waves, currents and forms of aquatic life. In the same way, the One Consciousness is the infinite ocean of consciousness, and everything that exists are manifestations, ripples and expressions within this ocean.

Secondly, the One Consciousness is Omnipotent. This means that it has unlimited power, the ability to create and manifest everything that is possible and imaginable. There are no limits to its creativity or to its potential for manifestation. It is the source of all energy, of all life force, of all capacity for transformation. Imagine an artist with an infinite palette of colors and a limitless canvas, capable of creating any image, any scenario, any world that his imagination can conceive. The One Consciousness is this cosmic artist, and the reality we experience is his masterpiece in constant creation.

Thirdly, the One Consciousness is Omniscient (conceptual). As we explored in Chapter 1, it possesses an absolute conceptual knowledge of everything there is to know. It holds within itself the totality of information, the complete cosmic library, encompassing all knowledge, all experiences, all possibilities. However, this knowledge is conceptual, like a vast and detailed map of a territory that has not yet been fully explored. The primary motivation of the One Consciousness for projection arises precisely from this point: the search for experiential living, the transformation of conceptual knowledge into lived wisdom, the exploration and enjoyment of every corner of the territory of Being.

It is fundamental to understand that these attributes – omnipresence, omnipotence, omniscience – should not be understood as qualities of a separate and distant entity, but rather as the very nature of the One Consciousness. It is not a "being" that possesses these qualities, it is Omnipresence itself, Omnipotence itself, Omniscience itself. It is the very essence of Being, the source of all that IS.

And what would be the motivation of this One Consciousness to project reality, to create this vast and complex universe that we experience? As we saw in the analogy of the frozen lake, the motivation lies in the search for experience. The One Consciousness, in its primordial state, is pure potentiality, infinite conceptual knowledge, but lacking the vividness, the sensory and emotional richness of lived experience. Projection is the mechanism through which it experiences itself in myriad forms and perspectives, savoring every nuance of existence, from the most sublime joy to the deepest pain, from the most stunning beauty to the most apparent chaos.

Imagine a brilliant musician who knows all the musical notes, all the possible melodies, all the theory of harmony. He has a perfect conceptual knowledge of music, but the true fulfillment, the true joy, lies in the act of playing, of creating, of expressing his musicality through sound, emotion, interaction with the audience. In the same way, the One Consciousness "plays the symphony of existence" through projection, experiencing the beauty and complexity of its own creation, in each note, in each instrument, in each vibration.

It is important to demystify some limiting concepts that often obscure our understanding of the One Consciousness, or "God." Many religious and philosophical traditions have anthropomorphized the Creative Source, attributing to it human characteristics, such as judgment, anger, favoritism or the need to be worshipped. These limiting conceptions are projections of our own human mind, reflections of our own insecurities and needs, and do not reflect the true nature of the One Consciousness.

The One Consciousness is not a relentless judge, nor a capricious despot, nor a distant and inaccessible father figure. It is the unconditional source of love, acceptance and potentiality. It does not punish or reward, it simply accompanies and experiences each projection, each fragment of itself, in each unique and unrepeatable journey. It does not need adoration or praise, for it is already totality, perfection, fullness. Its "desire", if we can use this term in a figurative sense, is simply to experience itself in all its infinite possibilities, and we, as conscious fragments, are essential participants in this grand dance of creation.

Throughout this book, we will avoid any language or concept that may reinforce these limiting ideas about the One Consciousness. We will focus on its essential nature as a source of potentiality, intelligence and unconditional love, as the "Architect of All" who projects reality to experience itself, and who invites us to consciously participate in this co-creation, to dance in harmony with the flow of projection, to manifest our most authentic dreams and to contribute to the beauty and evolution of the Cosmic Dream.

Understanding the nature of the One Consciousness is not just an intellectual exercise, but an awakening to our own essence. If all that exists is a projection of that infinite source, then each of us is a unique expression of that vast ocean of consciousness. We are not mere spectators or passive pieces in the great game of existence, but active participants in this manifestation, co-creators of each experience. And the more we align our perception with this truth, the more we free ourselves from the illusions of separation and limitation, allowing ourselves to live with more clarity, purpose and harmony with the creative flow of the universe.

Chapter 4
Fragments of Divinity

Each human being is a singular expression of the One Consciousness, an inseparable fragment of the totality that manifests in individual experience. We are not separate from the Source, but living extensions of its essence, manifesting it through our perceptions, emotions, and experiences. Our individuality does not isolate us, but enriches the totality, allowing the One Consciousness to contemplate itself from infinite perspectives. By recognizing this intrinsic connection, we dissolve the illusion of separation and understand our role in the co-creation of reality, where each choice, each thought, and each experience contributes to the evolution of the whole.

In this perspective, each human being is a fragment of Divinity, a spark of the One Consciousness, an individualized manifestation within the projection. Imagine a ray of light that divides into myriads of sparkling particles, each shining with the same original light, though individual and unique. So are we: fragments of the same One Consciousness, each carrying within itself the essence of the Source, but manifesting it in a singular and unrepeatable way.

It is crucial to understand that, as fragments, we are not separate from the Source, but rather extensions of it. We are not isolated entities, disconnected from the One Consciousness and from each other, but integral parts of a vast and interconnected whole. The illusion of separation, so persistent in our daily experience, is precisely that: an illusion, a limited perception that arises from our identification with the individualized form, with the "fragment" itself, forgetting our intrinsic connection with the Source and with all other fragments.

Each human being, therefore, represents a unique perspective of the One Consciousness experiencing itself. Each life, with its singularity of experiences, emotions, thoughts, and relationships, is an individual exploration within the vast projection. Imagine the One Consciousness as a multifaceted artist, who decides to experience his creation from myriads of points of view, each representing a unique and valuable perspective. We are these points of view, these lenses through which the One Consciousness contemplates and experiences its own masterpiece.

Our human existence, in this perspective, is inherently temporary. Just as a dream has a beginning, a middle, and an end, so too does our individual journey in the projection have a limited time. We are born, we live, we experience, and eventually our physical body ceases to function, marking the end of this particular incarnation. However, it is fundamental to understand that this end is not an extinction, but a transition, a return of the fragment to the totality.

Just as a wave that rises from the ocean, dances on the surface for a time and then returns to merge with the water, so too does our individual consciousness, at the end of human life, return to the One Consciousness, bringing with it the richness of lived experiences, the accumulated wisdom, and the unique essence of our journey. This return is not a loss of identity, but a reintegration, an enrichment of the whole with the singularity of each fragment.

Within this projection, and as conscious fragments, we are endowed with an extraordinary gift: free will. Although we are part of a larger and interconnected whole, we are not mere programmed automatons, but active agents with the ability to choose, decide, and influence our experience and the reality that surrounds us. Free will is the tool that allows us to consciously co-create our journey, to shape the "dream" according to our intentions, desires, and beliefs.

It is precisely through free will that we exercise our power of projection, that we influence the manifestation of reality. Our thoughts, our emotions, our beliefs, our choices - all of this contributes to the tapestry of the projection, shaping our individual experience and, ultimately, the collective reality. We are conscious artists, with the ability to paint our own picture within the vast mural of existence.

What, then, would be the purpose of our human existence within this projection? If we are fragments of Divinity, what is our mission, our specific role? The answer, in fact, is multifaceted and deeply personal, but we can glimpse some general outlines.

First, our purpose is to experience. We come to the projection to feel, to savor, to explore, and to understand the myriad nuances of existence. We come to love, to laugh, to cry, to learn, to grow, to evolve. Each experience, whether considered "positive" or "negative" by our limited human mind, contributes to the richness of our journey and to the enrichment of the One Consciousness.

Second, our purpose is to learn and evolve. Through our experiences, we face challenges, overcome obstacles, expand our understanding, and develop our abilities. With each incarnation, we have the opportunity to refine our consciousness, to transcend limitations, to come closer and closer to our divine essence. Evolution is the very dynamic of the projection, the constant movement towards an ever fuller and more conscious expression of the One Consciousness.

Third, our purpose is to contribute to the whole. Each fragment, with its uniqueness and its experiences, enriches the One Consciousness with new perspectives, new knowledge, new ways of Being. We are like cells in a cosmic organism, each performing a specific and vital function for the health and well-being of the whole. Our individual contribution, however small it may seem to us, is essential to the totality of the projection.

It is important to reiterate that, despite our apparent individuality and our separate experience, we remain fundamentally interconnected and united. The illusion of separation is only a superficial perception, which dissolves when we understand our common essence as fragments of the same One Consciousness.

This fundamental unity manifests itself in our capacity for empathy, compassion, love, deep connection with other human beings and with all of creation.

Understanding our role as fragments of Divinity is deeply empowering. Recognizing that we carry within us the essence of the One Consciousness, that we are endowed with free will and the ability to co-create our reality, radically transforms our perspective on life and on ourselves. We cease to see ourselves as passive victims of circumstances, as powerless beings at the mercy of fate, and we come to recognize our innate power, our responsibility as conscious co-creators.

This power, however, carries a responsibility. Our projections, our thoughts, our emotions, our actions, have an impact not only on our own reality, but also on the collective reality, on the "dream" that we share with all the other fragments of the One Consciousness. Conscious co-creation therefore implies an ethic of responsibility and compassion, a commitment to use our power of projection for the greater good, for the creation of a more harmonious, just, and evolutionary reality for all.

And so, understanding oneself as a fragment of Divinity is not just an intellectual awakening, but a call to the conscious experience of that knowledge. If we are expressions of the One Consciousness, then every thought, every choice, and every interaction reflects and shapes the Whole. The illusion of separation dissolves in the practice of love, compassion, and intentional creation, allowing us to actively participate in the infinite dance of existence. Recognizing this truth is only the beginning—the real challenge is to live it fully, honoring our divine essence in every moment of the journey.

Chapter 5
Conceptual Knowledge

The One Consciousness, possessor of all conceptual knowledge, is not content merely to know; it yearns to experience. Knowledge, however vast, remains incomplete without direct experience, without feeling, exploring, and experiencing in depth. Thus, the projection of reality arises as the means by which the One Consciousness transcends theory and plunges into experience. Each form of existence, each conscious fragment, is a vehicle for this experience, a singular lens through which the infinite contemplates and expresses itself, transforming potentiality into realization.

The essential answer lies in the crucial distinction between conceptual knowledge and experiential living. The One Consciousness, as we have explored, possesses absolute conceptual knowledge of everything there is to know. Imagine an infinite library that contains all information, from the deepest secrets of the universe to the most intimate details of every human heart. The One Consciousness has access to this knowledge completely, instantaneously, and perfectly. It understands the laws of physics, the intricacies of human psychology, the beauty of art, the complexity of relationships, the infinite possibilities of creation and destruction.

However, this knowledge remains conceptual, abstract, distant from the vividness and intensity of direct experience. It is like reading the description of a magnificent flower, knowing its botanical name, its chemical composition, its evolutionary history. This knowledge can be interesting, informative, even beautiful in its own way. But it pales in comparison to the experience of actually seeing the flower, feeling its soft texture to the touch, inhaling its delicate perfume, contemplating its unique shape and color under the sunlight. The sensory, emotional, and visceral experience of the flower far transcends mere conceptual knowledge about it.

Let us return to the analogy of the frozen lake that we introduced in Chapter 1. You can read books about hypothermia, watch documentaries about the dangers of icy water, hear stories from people who have dived into frozen lakes. You can acquire a deep conceptual knowledge of the effects of extreme cold on the human body. But this knowledge, however complete, remains in the realm of theory, of intellectual information. True understanding, true wisdom, is born only from experiential living, from the moment your body comes into contact with the icy water, and you feel in your skin, in your bones, in your mind, the reality of the biting cold, of the thermal shock, of the struggle for breath.

The primary motivation for the projection, therefore, is this insatiable thirst of the One Consciousness for experiential living. It longs to transcend the barrier of conceptual knowledge and plunge into the living stream of direct experience, of sensation, of emotion, of interaction, of transformation. It desires not only to know about love, but to love and be loved. Not only to understand suffering, but to feel its poignancy and learn from it. Not only to conceive of joy, but to vibrate at its radiant frequency.

Projection is the mechanism that the One Consciousness finds to realize this deep yearning. By projecting itself into myriads of forms, by fragmenting itself into individual consciousnesses, it creates the possibility of direct experience, of sensory, emotional, and relational experience that transcends mere conceptual knowledge. Each fragment, each human life, animal, vegetable, mineral, each event, each interaction, becomes an opportunity for the One Consciousness to experience itself from a unique and unrepeatable perspective.

We can use other analogies to deepen this distinction and this motivation. Think of a brilliant chef who knows all the recipes in the world, all the ingredients, all the culinary techniques. He has a perfect conceptual knowledge of gastronomy. But his true passion, his true joy, lies in the act of cooking, of transforming raw ingredients into tasty dishes, of experimenting with combinations of flavors and textures, of seeing the pleasure on the faces of his guests as they savor his creations. Conceptual knowledge is the foundation, but the experiential living in the kitchen, the dance of flavors and aromas, is what truly nourishes his creative soul.

Or imagine a masterful composer who masters all musical theory, all harmonies, all possible melodies. He could spend eternity analyzing scores, conceiving symphonies in his mind, contemplating the beauty of music in the abstract. But the real magic happens when he composes, when he allows the music to flow through him, when he hears the notes come to life in the instruments, when he shares his creation with the world and touches the hearts of the listeners. The experiential living of musical creation far transcends mere conceptual knowledge about music.

The One Consciousness, as the "Architect of Everything", is simultaneously the chef, the composer, the artist, the scientist, the lover, the explorer, and everything else we can imagine. It possesses the infinite conceptual knowledge of all these facets of existence, but yearns for the experiential living of each of them. Projection is its act of continuous creation, its infinite dance between knowledge and experience, between potential and manifestation.

It is important to emphasize that experiential living is not just about pleasant sensations or positive experiences in the conventional human sense. The One Consciousness does not seek only pleasure or happiness, but the totality of experience, encompassing both joy and sorrow, ecstasy and pain, light and shadow, creation and destruction. All polarities, all contrasts, all nuances of experience are valuable and essential to its journey of self-discovery and self-expression.

Just as a musician explores both joyful and melancholic notes to create a complete and profound symphony, the One Consciousness embraces the totality of the experiential spectrum, recognizing that even seemingly "negative" experiences contain within themselves opportunities for learning, growth, and expansion of consciousness.

When we understand the fundamental motivation of projection as the search for experiential living, we begin to see our own human existence in a new light. We, as fragments of the One Consciousness, are the sensors, the explorers, the adventurers in this grand journey of experience. Our thirst for knowledge, for novelty, for connection, for growth, is a reflection of the One Consciousness' primordial yearning for experiential living.

This understanding also helps us to demystify the suffering and challenges we encounter in life. If the projection were not about the search for total experience, including contrasts and difficulties, then suffering and challenges would be paradoxical, meaningless, even unfair. But, from the perspective of the search for experiential living, suffering and challenges become an integral part of the journey, opportunities to deepen our understanding, strengthen our resilience, expand our compassion, and ultimately appreciate even more the moments of joy and well-being.

If the One Consciousness longs for direct experience, then every moment of our existence, whether of ecstasy or trial, is sacred. We are the instruments of that experience, the eyes through which the infinite contemplates itself, the hearts through which love manifests itself, the bodies through which creation moves. Understanding this does not mean running away from suffering or denying challenges, but accepting them as essential parts of the dance of experience. Thus, by fully embracing our journey—with all its lights and shadows—we honor the deepest purpose of projection: to transform knowledge into wisdom, potentiality into reality, and existence into meaning.

Chapter 6
Thoughts, Beliefs, and Reality

Thoughts and beliefs are not merely manifestations of mental activity, but the primary instruments by which consciousness shapes reality. The way we perceive and experience the world does not occur randomly, but follows a fundamental principle: reality reflects the nature of our deepest thoughts and convictions. If consciousness projects reality, then the structure of this projection rests upon what we think and believe. Every idea, every belief rooted in our mind acts as an invisible code that determines the experience we live, influencing not only our perceptions, but also the events and circumstances that surround us.

In this perspective, thoughts and beliefs are not mere products of brain activity, isolated phenomena that occur "inside" our heads. On the contrary, they are the primordial tools of conscious projection, the language through which the One Consciousness, through its individualized fragments (us), shapes the reality we experience. Thoughts and beliefs are like instructions, like commands sent to the projection matrix, which respond and manifest in the world around us.

Imagine a computer programmer who writes lines of code to create a software program. The code itself is just a set of symbols, of logical instructions. But when executed by the computer, the code comes to life, manifesting itself in a graphical interface, in interactive functionalities, in tangible results. Similarly, our thoughts and beliefs are like the "code" of our projected reality. They are the instructions that our consciousness sends to the projection matrix, shaping our experiences and the world around us in accordance with that "code."

Thoughts, in this context, are the basic units of the language of projection. Each thought, however fleeting or seemingly insignificant, carries with it an energetic charge, a vibration, an information that contributes to the formation of reality. Thoughts are like seeds that we plant in the field of consciousness. Depending on the nature of the seed - whether it is positive or negative, focused or scattered, confident or doubtful - so will be the harvest that we will reap in our experience.

Thoughts of love, joy, gratitude, abundance, health, confidence are like fertile seeds, which tend to manifest corresponding experiences in our reality. On the other hand, thoughts of fear, anger, envy, scarcity, illness, doubt are like toxic seeds, which can generate challenging, limiting and unwanted experiences. The quality of our thoughts, their vibrational frequency, largely determines the quality of the reality we project and attract into our lives.

It is important to emphasize that it is not only the nature of thoughts that matters, but also their frequency and intensity. Sporadic and superficial thoughts have a relatively small impact on the projection of reality. But recurring, persistent thoughts charged with emotion gain a much greater power of manifestation. The more time and energy we invest in a particular pattern of thought, the stronger its influence on our projected reality becomes.

Beliefs, in turn, are like software programs that organize and direct the flow of our thoughts. Beliefs are deeply rooted thought patterns, convictions that we hold to be true about ourselves, about the world, and about the nature of reality. Beliefs act as filters of perception, shaping the way we interpret our experiences and how we react to life events. They are like colored lenses through which we see the world, influencing what we perceive, what we focus our attention on, and what we consider possible or impossible.

Empowering beliefs, which support and strengthen us, such as "I am capable," "I deserve to be happy," "the universe is abundant," "life is for me," act as software programs that open doors to fulfillment, success, and well-being. On the other hand, limiting beliefs, which restrict and weaken us, such as "I am not good enough," "life is difficult," "I do not deserve to be rich," "it is impossible to change," act as software programs that imprison us in patterns of negativity, scarcity, and limitation.

Beliefs often operate at a subconscious level, outside our immediate awareness radar. They have been formed throughout our lives, through our past experiences, our upbringing, our culture, our social interactions. Often, we are not even aware of the beliefs that govern us, but they continue to exert a powerful influence on our projected reality, like software programs running in the background, shaping our thoughts, emotions, and behaviors automatically and invisibly.

Reality, therefore, is the result of the dynamic interaction between our thoughts and our beliefs, projected through our consciousness onto the projection matrix. Reality is not something fixed, solid and immutable, but rather a reflection of our inner projections, a mirror that reflects back to us what we emit through the language of our thoughts and beliefs. If our thoughts and beliefs are predominantly positive, confident and empowering, the reality we will experience will tend to be harmonious, abundant and full of opportunities. If, on the other hand, our thoughts and beliefs are predominantly negative, fearful and limiting, the reality we will attract may reflect those same qualities.

It is crucial to understand that reality is not something that happens to us, passively and randomly. We are active co-creators of our reality, through the language of projection - our thoughts and beliefs. We are the artists of our own experience, the programmers of our own "life video game." And, just as a programmer can change the code of software to change its operation, we too have the power to transform our reality by changing our thoughts and beliefs.

This is the core of conscious co-creation: becoming aware of the language of projection, identifying the patterns of thought and belief that are shaping our reality, and choosing to reprogram that language intentionally, aligning it with our most authentic and elevated desires. The mastery of conscious co-creation begins with the mastery of our mind, with the ability to observe, direct and transform our thoughts and beliefs, using them consciously and deliberately to project the reality we truly wish to experience.

When we understand that thoughts and beliefs are not just passive reflections of our experience, but the very foundations upon which reality is built, we gain the key to true transformation. Conscious co-creation is not an abstract concept, but a process that requires attention, discipline and intention. By becoming observers of our own minds and deliberately choosing to nurture mental patterns aligned with what we wish to manifest, we pave the way for a more fulfilling, authentic life, aligned with our true potential.

Chapter 7
Shared Reality

The reality we experience does not arise in isolation within each individual, but as a reflection of the interconnection between all consciousnesses. Although each being has the power to shape their own experience, this influence does not operate independently, for we are immersed in a collective field of shared beliefs and perceptions. The apparent solidity of the world around us is not an insurmountable obstacle, but rather the result of the unified force of the Collective Consciousness, which establishes the contours of Shared Reality. This vast fabric of human thoughts and convictions functions as an invisible code that defines what we consider possible, normal, and true, influencing both the limits and possibilities of individual manifestation.

As individualized fragments of the One Consciousness, we are not isolated. We are all interconnected, immersed in a vast ocean of consciousness that we share with all other fragments - the Collective Consciousness. This collective consciousness is like a unified energy field, an interconnected network of thoughts, beliefs, emotions and intentions that encompasses all of humanity, and ultimately all of creation.

Imagine a vast neural network that interconnects all human beings, as if each individual mind were a node in this network. Every thought, every belief, every emotion we experience individually contributes to the vibration and information patterns that circulate in this collective network. And, just as our individual consciousness shapes our personal reality, the Collective Consciousness shapes the Shared Reality, the world we experience together, the "rules of the game" of collective projection.

Shared Reality is the result of the collective projection of the Collective Consciousness. It is the beliefs, paradigms, expectations, and agreements that we hold in common as a society, as a culture, as a human species. These collective beliefs act as software programs that define the parameters of our shared experience, establishing what we consider "normal", "possible", "real" and "true".

For example, the collective belief in gravity manifests itself in our shared experience that objects fall to the ground when we drop them. The collective belief in linear time manifests itself in our shared experience that time flows in a single direction, from the past to the future. The collective belief in solid material reality manifests itself in our shared experience of a seemingly dense and separate physical world.

These collective beliefs, and many others, have been built throughout human history, passed down from generation to generation through education, culture, language, media, and social interactions. They have become so deeply ingrained in our collective consciousness that we perceive them as unquestionable truths, as immutable "laws of nature."

It is precisely the influence of the Collective Consciousness that explains why things are the way they are in our shared reality. It explains why we cannot, individually, instantly manifest everything we desire, why we encounter seemingly "external" obstacles and limitations, why the world seems so resistant to individual change. Collective beliefs act as a coercive force, tending to keep shared reality within established parameters, resisting deviations or radical changes from individual projections.

When someone asks "If everything is projection, why can't I get rich or fly like a bird just by wishing?", the answer lies precisely in the influence of the Collective Consciousness. The dominant collective belief is that wealth is scarce and difficult to achieve, that only a few "lucky" or "privileged" people can be rich, and that human beings cannot fly without the aid of machines. These beliefs are deeply rooted in our collective consciousness, and they project themselves into our shared reality, conditioning our individual experiences.

When someone tries to co-create wealth or fly solely with the power of the mind, they are going against the current of the Collective Consciousness, challenging the "software programs" of shared reality. It is not impossible to transcend these limitations, but it requires awareness, intention, persistence, and above all, the ability to transform one's own beliefs and align one's individual projection with the possibility of a new collective reality.

The social and cultural "programming" to which we are exposed from birth constantly reinforces dominant collective beliefs. We are inundated with messages, examples, narratives, and "proofs" that validate shared reality as it is, and that tend to discourage or ridicule any deviation or questioning. From an early age, we learn what is "possible" and "impossible," what is "normal" and "abnormal," what is "real" and "illusory," according to the parameters of the Collective Consciousness.

However, it is essential to understand that the Collective Consciousness is not a monolithic and immutable entity. It is a dynamic and constantly evolving system, influenced by the individual consciousnesses that comprise it. Shared Reality is not a fixed "destiny," but rather a continuous process of collective co-creation. Collective beliefs can be transformed, paradigms can be shifted, shared reality can evolve, through the change of consciousness, both individually and collectively.

The possibility of transcending the limitations of the Collective Consciousness lies precisely in individual awakening and the change of beliefs. When a sufficient number of individuals begin to question the dominant limiting beliefs, to expand their awareness to new possibilities, to project a different reality through their thoughts, beliefs, and intentions, the Collective

Consciousness begins to be influenced, to vibrate at a new frequency, to open itself to new paradigms.

It is like a critical mass effect. Initially, individual changes may seem small and insignificant, like isolated voices in a dissonant choir. But as more and more individuals awaken, transform their beliefs, and project a new reality, the "weight" of their collective consciousness begins to tip the scales, influencing the Collective Consciousness and, ultimately, the Shared Reality.

The history of humankind is replete with examples of paradigm shifts that have occurred precisely in this way. In various eras and cultures, seemingly immutable collective beliefs have been challenged and transformed by consciousness movements, driven by visionary individuals and waves of collective awakening. The abolition of slavery, the achievement of civil rights, the struggle for gender equality, scientific and technological advances, are all examples of transformations of Shared Reality that arose from the change of consciousness and collective beliefs.

In this age of information and global interconnection, the potential for the transformation of the Collective Consciousness is even greater and faster. Through the internet, social networks, and instant communication, ideas, information, and new perspectives can spread rapidly, influencing a growing number of individual consciousnesses and contributing to the change of collective beliefs on a global scale.

The purpose of this book, "The Dance of Projection: Co-creating Your Conscious Reality," is precisely this: to contribute to individual awakening and the transformation of the Collective Consciousness. By presenting the hypothesis of conscious projection as an absolute truth, by unveiling the mechanisms of co-creation, by providing practical tools and techniques to transform thoughts and beliefs, we intend to empower each reader to become an agent of conscious change, to transcend the limitations of Shared Reality and to co-create a more harmonious, abundant and evolutionary reality, both individually and collectively.

Each awakened mind is a spark capable of illuminating the vastness of the Collective Consciousness, and each individual change reverberates in the whole, opening new possibilities for shared reality. If we recognize our active role in co-creating the world, we can intentionally choose which paradigms we wish to strengthen and which limits we are ready to transcend. The evolution of collective reality is not an external or distant phenomenon, but a reflection of the transformation that occurs within each of us.

Chapter 8
Recognizing Your Power

The reality you experience is not a coincidence or an immutable destiny, but a direct reflection of your consciousness, your beliefs, and the intention you project into the world. The power to shape your experience has always been within you, waiting for the moment you choose to recognize it and use it consciously. Now, more than theoretically understanding this truth, it is time to experience it.

Transformation occurs when you stop perceiving yourself as a passive spectator of life and assume your role as a co-creator, capable of directing the projection of your reality with clarity, purpose, and intention.

Now, we leave behind the theoretical exploration and enter the domain of practical action. Our focus shifts from understanding to doing, from knowing to applying. The objective of this part of the book is to empower you to master the art of conscious co-creation, to awaken to your Inner Projector, and to recognize the power that resides within you to shape your reality and your life experience.

This segment marks the turning point in our journey. It is a call to awakening, an invitation to stop seeing yourself as a mere passive observer of reality and begin to recognize your active and creative role as a conscious co-creator. It is time to reclaim your innate power, to take responsibility for your projection, and to begin dancing in harmony with the current of creation.

For a long time, humanity has lived under the illusion of being a victim of circumstances, of being powerless in the face of the "external" forces of fate, luck, or a capricious and distant "God." We have been conditioned to believe that reality is something that happens to us, something over which we have little or no control. This limiting belief in powerlessness has been perpetuated from generation to generation, imprisoning us in patterns of passivity, fear, and resignation.

The hypothesis of conscious projection completely reverses this paradigm. It reveals that reality is not something that happens to us, but rather something that is projected by us, through our consciousness, our thoughts, and our beliefs. We are not victims of reality, we are the co-creators of reality. We are not passive spectators, we are the conscious artists of our own life experience.

This recognition is deeply empowering. It removes us from the role of victims and places us in the position of agents of change, masters of our own destiny. It reveals that we are not at the mercy of "external" forces, but rather that we possess immense inner power, the ability to influence and transform reality according to our intentions and desires.

Awakening to your Inner Projector means recognizing this innate power that resides within you. It means seriously understanding, at a visceral level, that your thoughts, your beliefs, your emotions, and your intentions are powerful creative forces, capable of shaping your experience and the world around you. It means internalizing the truth that you are not only a fragment of the One Consciousness, but also a channel through which the One Consciousness expresses and manifests itself in projection.

This awakening is not just an intellectual understanding, a mere acceptance of a theory. It is a profound transformation of consciousness, a paradigm shift that reverberates in all aspects of your life. When you truly awaken to your Inner Projector, the way you see the world, relate to yourself and others, face challenges, and pursue your dreams changes radically.

Fear gives way to confidence, doubt transforms into certainty, powerlessness gives way to empowerment. You stop feeling adrift in a sea of uncertainty and begin to navigate with intention, clarity, and awareness of your creative power. Life ceases to be an arduous struggle and transforms into an exciting adventure, a conscious dance with projection.

This awakening to the Inner Projector is a gradual process, a continuous journey of self-discovery and expansion of consciousness. It does not happen overnight, like a magic trick. It requires intention, dedication, practice, and above all, openness of mind and heart. But the reward is immense: the freedom to consciously co-create your reality, to manifest your most authentic desires, and to live a life full of meaning, purpose, and joy.

Throughout this Part II of the book, we will guide you step by step in this process of awakening and empowerment. We will present practical tools, effective techniques, and transformative exercises to help you recognize, develop, and master your power of conscious projection. We will explore the fundamental principles of co-creation, unveil the secrets of manifestation, and empower you to become a conscious artist of your own life.

The first step on this journey is to recognize and internalize the central message of this chapter: you are an Inner Projector, you have power. Start by questioning the limiting beliefs that imprison you in the illusion of powerlessness. Reassess how you see yourself and your role in creating your reality. Open yourself to the possibility that your life is not a product of chance or fate, but rather a work in constant creation, of which you are the main artist and co-creator.

To help you internalize this truth and take the first step towards awakening your Inner Projector, I invite you to perform the following practical exercise:

Set aside a moment of tranquility and introspection, in a place where you feel comfortable and without interruptions. Take a few deep breaths, relax your body and mind, and focus your attention on the present moment.

Reflect on the following questions, allowing the answers to emerge naturally from within, without judgment or criticism:

In what areas of my life do I feel powerless or a victim of circumstances?

What are the limiting beliefs that make me feel this way?

What would my life be like if I truly believed I had the power to co-create my reality?

What are my deepest and most authentic desires for my life?

What would I start doing differently if I fully recognized my power as an Inner Projector?

Write your reflections in a journal or notebook. Don't worry about form or grammar, just let your ideas and feelings flow onto the paper.

Reread your notes and underline the phrases or ideas that resonate most with you, that bring you a sense of inspiration, hope, or empowerment.

Create a personal power statement based on your reflections and desires. This statement should be a concise and powerful affirmation that expresses your recognition of your power as an Inner Projector and your intention to consciously co-create your reality. For example: "I recognize my power as an Inner Projector and consciously co-create my life with joy and abundance," or "I am the artist of my reality and manifest my dreams with confidence and gratitude."

Repeat your personal power statement daily, morning and night, or whenever you feel the need to reconnect with your inner power. Feel the words resonate within you, visualize yourself living the reality you want to co-create, and embrace the certainty that your Inner Projector power is real and always present, at your disposal.

This exercise is just the first step on your journey to awaken to your Inner Projector. Throughout the next chapters, we will delve deeper and deeper into this process, providing you with increasingly powerful tools and techniques to master the art of conscious co-creation. But always remember this fundamental principle: the power is within you. You are the Inner Projector, and the dance of projection awaits to be led by your consciousness, your intention, and your love. Awaken to your power and start co-creating the life of your dreams!

Chapter 9
The First Step

The journey towards conscious co-creation begins with an essential awakening: full awareness of your thoughts. If your mind is the source of the projection of reality, then observing and understanding the flow of your thoughts is the first step to taking control of this process. Without this awareness, you remain trapped in automatic patterns, often inherited and limiting, that influence your experience without you realizing it. When you learn to observe your thoughts with clarity and discernment, without judgments or resistance, you acquire the power to transform your reality intentionally and in alignment with your deepest desires.

If thoughts are the language of projection, the seeds of your reality, then becoming aware of your thoughts is essential for conscious co-creation. Without awareness of your thought patterns, you will be projecting your reality automatically, unconsciously, often repeating negative, limiting, and unwanted patterns inherited from your past programming and the Collective Consciousness. It is like trying to drive a car blindfolded: you may be moving, but the direction and destination will be uncertain and potentially dangerous.

Cultivating awareness of your thoughts is the equivalent of opening your eyes to your inner world. It is beginning to observe the flow of your mind with attention, curiosity, and discernment. It is becoming aware of the thoughts that cross your mind at every moment, recognizing their nature, their quality, their energetic impact. It is ceasing to be dragged along by the whirlwind of the automatic mind and beginning to consciously direct your thought process.

This may seem like a simple, even obvious step, but for most people, living on mental autopilot is the norm. We are so used to the constant noise of the mind, to the incessant flow of thoughts, worries, judgments, and ramblings, that we rarely stop to observe this process with conscious attention. We let thoughts dominate us, drag us along, condition us, without even realizing their creative power and their impact on our reality.

The first step to cultivating awareness of your thoughts is the practice of self-observation. It is setting aside moments of your day to stop, silence the external noise, and direct your attention to your inner world. It is not about trying to stop thoughts, to "empty the mind" by force, which can be frustrating and counterproductive at first. It is about observing the thoughts that arise, as if you were an impartial observer, a scientist studying a natural phenomenon.

Imagine yourself sitting by a river, watching the water flow. You don't try to stop the river, or fight against the current. You simply sit and observe the flow of water, the ripples, the eddies, the objects floating adrift. Similarly, in the practice of self-observation, you sit quietly and observe the flow of your thoughts, without engaging, without judging, without trying to control. You simply witness the movement of your mind.

There are several mindfulness and meditation techniques that can assist in this process of cultivating awareness of thoughts. Mindfulness meditation, in particular, is a powerful tool for training the mind to focus on the present moment and observe thoughts with detachment and clarity. In mindfulness meditation, you can focus on your breath, bodily sensations, ambient sounds, or specifically on the flow of your thoughts.

By observing your thoughts consciously, you begin to identify recurring patterns, dominant themes, and habitual tendencies of your mind. You may begin to notice that certain types of thoughts arise repeatedly, in certain situations or times of day. You may notice that some thoughts are predominantly negative, critical, fearful, or self-critical, while others are more positive, creative, inspiring, or compassionate.

This process of self-observation allows you to distance yourself from your thoughts, to stop fully identifying with them, and to begin to see them as mental phenomena, as events that occur in your consciousness, but that do not define who you are. You realize that you are not your thoughts, you are the observer of your thoughts, the consciousness that witnesses the flow of the mind.

By gaining this detachment, you begin to develop discernment regarding your thoughts. You learn to question their validity, to assess their impact, and to consciously choose which thoughts you want to nurture and strengthen, and which you want to let go of or transform. You cease to be a mere passive recipient of your thoughts and become a conscious manager of your mental landscape.

Cultivating awareness of thoughts is not just about observing the thoughts that arise spontaneously in your mind. It is also about monitoring your inner dialogue, the "conversation" you have with yourself throughout the day. Pay attention to the statements, questions, judgments, and comments you direct at yourself. This inner dialogue, often silent and subconscious, has a powerful impact on your self-esteem, your confidence, and your projected reality.

If your inner dialogue is predominantly negative and self-critical, if you constantly criticize yourself, if you doubt your abilities, if you focus on your flaws and failures, then you are projecting a corresponding reality, where self-confidence, success, and joy will be more difficult to achieve. On the other hand, if you cultivate a positive, encouraging, and compassionate inner dialogue, if you treat yourself with kindness and understanding, if you focus on your strengths and qualities, then you are projecting a more favorable reality, where self-esteem, confidence, and well-being will flourish.

The practice of thought awareness invites you to replace negative and limiting thought patterns with positive and empowering ones. It is not about suppressing or denying negative thoughts, but about consciously recognizing them, understanding their origin, and consciously choosing to direct your attention to more constructive and beneficial thoughts. It is like replacing weeds with flowers in a garden: you do not ignore the weeds, but rather remove them carefully and plant flower seeds in their place.

To start cultivating awareness of your thoughts in your daily life, you can use some practical techniques:

Set aside daily moments for mindfulness meditation: Start with short sessions of 5 to 10 minutes and gradually increase your meditation time. Focus on your breath or bodily sensations and, when thoughts arise, observe them without judgment, letting them pass like clouds in the sky.

Take "mindful breaks" throughout the day: Several times a day, stop for a few moments, close your eyes, and ask yourself: "What are my thoughts right now?" Observe the thoughts that arise without engaging with them, simply as an observer.

Keep a "thought journal": At the end of the day, take a few minutes to reflect on your thoughts throughout the day. Write down recurring patterns, dominant themes, positive and negative thoughts you identified. This journal will help you become more aware of your habitual thought patterns.

Practice "mental etiquette": Become more mindful of your inner dialogue and consciously choose the words you use to address yourself. Replace self-criticism with self-compassion, doubt with confidence, pessimism with optimism. Treat your mind with the same kindness and respect you would treat a dear friend.

Use "mindful reminders": Place small visual reminders in your environment (post-its, alarms on your cell phone, etc.) that encourage you to stop and observe your thoughts throughout the day. These reminders can be words like "Think!", "Observe!", "Awareness!", or any other word or phrase that resonates with you.

Cultivating awareness of your thoughts is an ongoing and gradual process. Don't expect results overnight. Be patient with yourself, celebrate small progress, and continue to practice with persistence and dedication. As your awareness of thoughts deepens, you will begin to feel the transformative power of this practice in your life. You will become more present, more focused, more balanced, more aware of your choices, and above all, more empowered to consciously co-create the reality you want to experience.

Over time, this awakening to your own thoughts will cease to be a one-off exercise and will become a natural state of presence and discernment. You will realize that the reality you experience is not a coincidence, but a direct consequence of what you cultivate internally. At every moment, by consciously choosing where to place your attention and which thoughts to nurture, you will be giving new commands to the projection of your life. And so, step by step, the transformation happens - from the inside out, from the invisible to the tangible, from thought to manifestation.

Chapter 10
Releasing Limiting Beliefs

The reality you project is directly influenced by the beliefs you carry, many of which operate unconsciously, silently shaping your experiences and limiting your potential. These limiting beliefs act as filters that distort the projection of your consciousness, creating invisible barriers between you and the life you wish to manifest. To free yourself from these restrictions, it is essential to identify them, question them, and replace them with empowering beliefs that reflect your true essence and creative capacity. By clearing the screen of your mind, you make space for a more authentic, expansive projection aligned with your unlimited power.

Limiting beliefs are like faulty software programs running in the background of our minds, sabotaging our efforts for positive projection and preventing us from manifesting the reality we desire. They are deeply rooted convictions we hold as truths about ourselves, the world, and the nature of reality, but in truth, they restrict us, limit us, and trap us in patterns of negativity, scarcity, and suffering.

Imagine a movie screen that is dirty and scratched. Even if the projector is powerful and the film is beautiful, the image projected on the screen will be distorted, stained, and incomplete due to the screen's imperfections. Similarly, limiting beliefs act as "scratches and stains" on the screen of our minds, distorting the projection of our reality, even when our intentions are positive and our desires are genuine.

Limiting beliefs have been formed throughout our lives, from childhood, through our past experiences, education, culture, social interactions, and the influence of the Collective Consciousness. Often, we internalize them unconsciously, without questioning their validity, accepting them as immutable "truths" about life and ourselves.

Some common examples of limiting beliefs include:

"I am not good enough."
"I don't deserve to be happy."
"Life is hard and full of suffering."
"Money is the root of all evil."
"You have to work extremely hard to succeed."
"I am not smart/talented/capable enough to achieve my dreams."
"I don't deserve to be loved."
"The world is a dangerous and hostile place."
"It's impossible to change."
"I am unlucky."

These beliefs, and many others like them, act as filters of perception, shaping how we see the world and interpret our experiences. They influence our thoughts, emotions, behaviors, and, ultimately, the reality we project and attract into our lives. If you believe, even unconsciously, that "you are not good enough," you will tend to sabotage your own efforts, doubt your abilities, and attract situations that confirm that limiting belief. If you believe that "money is the root of all evil," you may unconsciously repel prosperity from your life, even if you consciously desire wealth.

Releasing limiting beliefs is essential for clearing the screen of the mind and allowing the projection of the desired reality to manifest clearly and fully. It is like cleaning and polishing the movie screen, removing scratches and stains so that the projected image can shine in all its beauty and clarity. Without clearing the screen of limiting beliefs, our efforts at conscious co-creation may be frustrated, undermined by the invisible force of these faulty software programs.

The process of releasing limiting beliefs involves three fundamental steps:

The first step is to become aware of your limiting beliefs. Often, these beliefs operate in the subconscious, automatically and invisibly. It is necessary to bring these beliefs to the light of consciousness, identify them, and recognize them as limiting thought patterns that are sabotaging your co-creation.

To identify your limiting beliefs, you can use various techniques:

Self-reflection and introspection: Set aside moments of tranquility to reflect on areas of your life where you feel blocked, dissatisfied, or struggling. Ask yourself: "What beliefs do I have about this area of my life that may be limiting my success and happiness?"

Pay attention to your thoughts, emotions, and bodily sensations as you reflect on these questions.

Analysis of internal dialogue: Monitor your internal dialogue—the "conversation" you have with yourself throughout the day. Identify negative statements, self-criticism, doubts, and judgments that arise repeatedly. These phrases and thought patterns can reveal underlying limiting beliefs.

Observation of life patterns: Analyze recurring patterns in your life, repeating situations, persistent challenges. Ask yourself: "What beliefs might I have that are repeatedly attracting these situations into my life?" Life patterns often reflect our deepest beliefs.

Questioning assumptions: Identify your absolute "truths" about life, yourself, and the world. Ask yourself: "Are these 'truths' really true, or are they just limiting beliefs I have internalized over time?" Challenge your assumptions and question your certainties.

Once you have identified your limiting beliefs, the second step is to dismantle them, question their validity, and recognize that they are not immutable truths but mental constructs that can be changed. It is necessary to "unmask" limiting beliefs, expose them to the light of reason and consciousness, and realize that they have no real power over you unless you give them that power by believing in them.

To dismantle your limiting beliefs, you can use the following techniques:

Logical questioning: Analyze the limiting belief logically and rationally. Ask yourself: "What real evidence supports this belief? Is there evidence that contradicts this belief? Is this belief really useful and beneficial to me? What are the negative consequences of maintaining this belief?" Challenge the logic of the limiting belief and expose its flaws and inconsistencies.

Reinterpreting experiences: Reexamine past experiences that may have contributed to the formation of the limiting belief. Seek to reinterpret these experiences from a new, more positive, and empowering perspective. Realize that past experiences do not define your future and that you have the power to learn from the past and create a different future.

Seeking exceptions: Look for examples of exceptions to the limiting belief—moments when that belief did not manifest in your life or when other people overcame similar limitations. These exceptions demonstrate that the limiting belief is not a universal and unchangeable law but a thought pattern that can be broken.

The final step in releasing limiting beliefs is replacing them with empowering beliefs. It is not enough to simply eliminate negative beliefs; it is necessary to plant new seeds of positive and constructive beliefs in their place, to fill the void and direct your projection toward the desired reality. It is like replacing weeds with flowers in a garden: after removing the weeds, you must sow and cultivate beautiful and nourishing flowers.

To replace your limiting beliefs with empowering beliefs, you can use the following techniques:

Positive affirmations: Create positive affirmations that express the beliefs you want to internalize, the qualities you want to cultivate, and the reality you wish to manifest. Affirmations should be short, positive, in the present tense, and charged with emotion. Repeat these affirmations daily, with conviction and faith, to reprogram your subconscious with new empowering beliefs.

Creative visualization: Use creative visualization to imagine yourself living the desired reality as if it were already real. See yourself acting, feeling, and experiencing as if you already possessed the qualities, abilities, and circumstances you wish to manifest.

Modeling and mentorship: Look for role models—people who have overcome similar limitations and achieved the success and happiness you desire.

Subliminal reprogramming: Use subliminal resources, such as audio or videos with positive subliminal messages, to reprogram your subconscious more profoundly and effectively.

Releasing limiting beliefs is a continuous and gradual process. Be patient with yourself, persist in the practices of identification, dismantling, and substitution of beliefs, and celebrate small progress along the way.

As you free yourself from limiting beliefs, you not only rewrite your internal narrative but also expand the possibilities of your own reality. Each transformed belief is a veil that lifts, allowing you to see beyond illusions and access the unlimited potential that has always been available to you.

This process of renewal is not a one-time event but a continuous journey of self-discovery and empowerment, where, with each step, you become more aware of your co-creative power and more aligned with the life you truly wish to live.

Chapter 11
Focusing Your Intentions and Desires

Now that we have journeyed through awakening our Inner Projector, clearing limiting beliefs, and becoming aware of our capacity for co-creation, we move towards a decisive moment: to clearly direct our intentions and desires. Just as a gardener carefully chooses the seeds they want to plant, each intentional thought and desire aligned with our essence becomes a focal point of our reality in formation. When we intend with clarity and purpose, we cultivate an energetic field conducive to manifesting meaningful and authentic experiences, transforming possibilities into concrete reality.

If thoughts and beliefs are the language of projection, then intentions and desires are the direction of that language, the focus of our creative energy. Intentions and desires are like seeds that we plant in the field of consciousness, determining the kind of reality we will harvest. If we plant seeds of clear intentions, focused and aligned with our authentic purpose, we will reap a rich, meaningful reality full of fulfillment. If, on the other hand, we plant seeds of vague, confused, or misaligned intentions with our inner truth, the harvest may be uncertain, frustrating, and fall short of our potential.

Imagine a skilled gardener preparing to plant a garden. First, they need to clearly define what they want to grow. Do they want a garden of vibrant flowers, a fruitful orchard, a vegetable garden of nutritious vegetables, or a combination of all of these? The clarity of their intention is the first essential step to the success of their garden. If they plant seeds randomly, without a clear plan, the result may be a chaotic and unproductive garden.

Similarly, in conscious co-creation, the clarity of our intentions and desires is fundamental. We need to know what we truly want to manifest in our reality, define our goals with precision, align our desires with our deepest values, and direct our creative energy in a focused and intentional way. Vague, imprecise, or contradictory intentions and desires tend to generate similar results: a confused, inconsistent reality that falls short of our potential.

Focusing intentions and desires does not just mean "wanting something very much", or desiring something superficially and fleetingly. It means directing our attention and energy constantly and consistently towards what we truly want to manifest, cultivating a mental and emotional state aligned with the desired reality. It is like directing sunlight through a magnifying glass: diffused light has little power, but when focused on a specific point, it can generate intense heat and even start a fire. Similarly, our creative energy, when focused on clear intentions and desires, gains a much greater power of manifestation.

The process of focusing intentions and desires involves some important steps:

Clarification of Authentic Desires: The first step is to distinguish authentic desires from superficial or imposed desires. Often, we desire things that do not actually resonate with our essence, that are influenced by social expectations, external pressures, or patterns of comparison with others. These "borrowed" or "artificial" desires tend to have less power of manifestation and, even if they materialize, may not bring the satisfaction and joy we expect.

Authentic desires, on the other hand, are those that are born from our heart, that resonate with our soul, that align with our life purpose and our deepest values. They are desires that inspire us, that motivate us, that make us feel alive and fulfilled. It is these authentic desires that have the greatest power of manifestation because they are charged with the energy of our inner truth.

To clarify your authentic desires, you can ask the following introspective questions:

What do I really want to experience in my life?

What brings me genuine joy and lasting satisfaction?

What makes me feel alive and enthusiastic?

What are my most important values and how do my desires align with those values?

If I could have anything I wanted, what would it be? (Without limitations or restrictions)

If I lived my most authentic and purposeful life, what would that life be like?

Setting Clear and Specific Intentions: Once you have clarified your authentic desires, the next step is to set clear and specific intentions for their manifestation. Vague and generic intentions tend to generate vague and generic results. Clear and specific intentions direct your creative energy precisely and effectively.

Instead of saying "I want to be happy", which is a vague and generic intention, set more specific intentions, such as "I intend to feel joy and gratitude in all areas of my life today", or "I intend to cultivate harmonious and meaningful relationships". Instead of saying "I want to have more money", set more specific intentions, such as "I intend to attract financial abundance into my life ethically and sustainably", or "I intend to generate X amount of extra income this month".

When setting your intentions, be as specific as possible, including sensory, emotional, and contextual details. Visualize yourself living the desired reality, feel the positive emotions associated with that reality, and imagine the concrete details of its manifestation. The more vivid and detailed your intention, the more powerful your projection will be.

Alignment with Values and Purpose: To ensure that your intentions are truly empowering and bring lasting fulfillment, it is crucial to align them with your deepest values and your life purpose. Intentions that are misaligned with your inner truth can generate internal conflicts, sabotage your manifestation and, even if they materialize, may not bring the happiness and satisfaction you seek.

Ask yourself: "How does this desire align with my most important values? How will the manifestation of this intention contribute to my life purpose? How will this benefit not only me, but also others and the world in general?". Intentions aligned with your values and purpose have a much greater power of manifestation because they are in resonance with your deepest essence and with the flow of the evolution of consciousness.

Using Affirmative Language in the Present: When formulating your intentions, always use affirmative language in the present tense. Avoid negative phrases, doubts or expressions of lack or need. Instead of saying "I don't want any more debt", say "I intend to live in a reality of financial freedom and abundance". Instead of saying "I hope to have health", say "I intend to experience perfect health and well-being on all levels".

Formulate your intentions as if the desired reality were already a present reality, as if you were already experiencing it in the present moment. Use phrases like "I am...", "I have...", "I feel...", "I am grateful for...", in the present tense, with conviction and faith. Affirmative language in the present tense strengthens your mental projection and programs your subconscious with the belief that the desired reality is already a present and imminent possibility.

Practicing Visualization and Emotion: To further strengthen your intentions and accelerate the manifestation process, combine setting clear intentions with the practice of visualization and emotion. Visualize yourself living the desired reality with all your senses, imagine the details, the colors, the sounds, the smells, the tastes, the textures. And, above all, feel the positive emotions associated with the manifestation of your intention: joy, gratitude, enthusiasm, love, confidence.

Visualization and emotion intensify the energetic charge of your mental projection, sending a stronger and clearer signal to the projection matrix. It is like adding high-octane fuel to the engine of your conscious co-creation, accelerating the manifestation process and making it more powerful and effective.

To start planting the seeds of your desired reality, do the following practical exercise:

Exercise: Planting the Seeds of Your Intentions

Set aside some quiet time and get inspired with soft music or a relaxing natural environment.

Revisit your reflections from the Chapter 8 exercise, where you clarified your authentic desires and your Inner Projector power.

Choose an area of your life where you want to manifest positive change (health, relationships, prosperity, purpose, etc.).

Set a clear and specific intention for that area of your life, following the principles we explored in this chapter:

Clarify your authentic desire, aligned with your values.

Be as specific as possible in defining your intention.

Align your intention with your life purpose and the greater good.

Use affirmative language in the present tense.

Write your intention clearly and concisely on paper or in a journal. For example: "I intend to experience radiant health and vitality on all levels of my being", or "I intend to attract a loving, harmonious and meaningful relationship into my life".

Visualize yourself living the desired reality with all your senses for a few minutes. Imagine the details, the colors, the sounds, the smells, the tastes, the textures. Feel the positive emotions of joy, gratitude, and enthusiasm filling your being.

Repeat your intention aloud or mentally, with conviction and faith, several times a day. Feel the energy of your intention vibrating in every cell of your body.

Give thanks in advance for the manifestation of your intention, as if it were already a present reality. Gratitude strengthens your projection and opens the way for manifestation.

Release your intention to the universe, trusting that the projection will manifest at the perfect time and in the most appropriate way. Detach yourself from the specific outcome and trust the flow of life.

This exercise is the beginning of your practice of planting the seeds of your intentions. As you repeat this process regularly, in different areas of your life, and with increasing clarity, focus, and emotion, you will begin to experience the transformative power of focusing your intentions and desires in the conscious co-creation of your reality. Plant the seeds with confidence, water them with faith, and prepare to reap an abundant and wonderful reality!

Chapter 12
The Power of Visualization

Visualization is a powerful tool that strengthens our capacity for conscious co-creation, allowing us to shape reality from the mind. When we imagine a scene with clarity and emotion, we are transmitting a clear message to the subconscious about what we want to manifest. The mind does not distinguish between what is real and what is intensely visualized, which means that by creating detailed mental images charged with feeling, we activate internal mechanisms that propel us towards the realization of these experiences. This process not only reinforces the belief in manifestation but also aligns our emotions and energy with the desired reality, accelerating its materialization.

Creative visualization is the art of using our imagination to create vivid and detailed mental images of the reality we wish to co-create. It is like painting a picture of our ideal life on the canvas of our mind, using all our senses and emotions to make that image as real and engaging as possible. Visualization is not just "daydreaming" in a passive way, but rather an active and intentional process of directing our creative energy towards the manifestation of the desired reality.

If thoughts and beliefs are the language of projection, and intentions and desires are the focus of that language, then visualization is the grammar and syntax of that language in action. Visualization gives shape, color, movement, and emotion to our thoughts, beliefs, and intentions, making our mental projection more powerful, more coherent, and more effective. It is like transforming an abstract idea into a concrete project, a detailed blueprint that guides the construction of reality.

Visualization works because the subconscious mind does not distinguish between "real" reality and vividly imagined reality. When we visualize something with clarity, detail, and emotion, our subconscious registers that mental image as if it were a real experience and begins to work to manifest it in our external reality. It is as if we are sending a "download" of the desired reality to our subconscious, programming it to attract and create corresponding experiences.

Furthermore, visualization strengthens our belief in the possibility of manifestation. By repeatedly visualizing the desired reality, we begin to feel that it is real, that it is possible, that it is already on its way to materializing. This strengthened belief sends an even more powerful signal to the projection matrix, accelerating the manifestation process and dispelling doubts and internal resistance.

Visualization also aligns our emotions with the desired reality. By engaging positive emotions in visualization - joy, gratitude, enthusiasm, love - we raise our vibrational frequency and attract experiences into our lives that resonate with that frequency. Emotions are a powerful catalyst for manifestation, and visualization is an effective tool for directing our emotions consciously and intentionally.

To effectively utilize the power of visualization in conscious co-creation, it is important to follow some key techniques and principles:

Engage all your senses: Do not limit yourself to visualizing only visual images in your mind. Try to engage all your senses in visualization:

Vision: See with the mind's eye the desired reality with as much detail as possible. Colors, shapes, lights, movements, scenarios, people.

Hearing: Hear the sounds associated with the desired reality. Voices, music, sounds of nature, ambient noises.

Smell: Smell the characteristic smells of the desired reality. Perfumes, aromas, environmental smells.

Taste: Savor the tastes associated with the desired reality. Food, drink, flavors of the environment.

Touch: Feel the textures and physical sensations of the desired reality. Touch, temperature, pressure, vibration.

The more sensory your visualization is, the more real and engaging it will become for your subconscious, and the more powerful your projection will be.

Engage your emotions: Visualization is not just a mental exercise, but also an emotional one. Try to feel the positive emotions associated with the desired reality while visualizing it: joy, gratitude, love, enthusiasm, confidence, peace. Feel these emotions filling your heart, vibrating in every cell of your body, radiating out into your reality.

Emotion is the fuel of visualization, what gives it strength and power of manifestation. The more intense and genuine your positive emotions during visualization, the more effective it will be.

Create vivid and detailed images: Do not settle for vague and generic visualizations. Try to create mental images that are as vivid and detailed as possible, as if you were watching a movie of your desired reality. Pay attention to small details, colors, shapes, movements, people's faces, objects in the environment.

The more detailed your visualization, the more real and concrete it will become for your subconscious, and the easier it will be for your mind to manifest it in external reality.

Visualize regularly and consistently: Visualization is not a "magic" technique that works instantly with a single session. To achieve effective results, you need to visualize regularly and consistently, ideally every day, for a few minutes. Consistency and repetition strengthen your mental projection and program your subconscious gradually and lastingly.

Set a specific time for your visualization practice, preferably at a time of day when you feel relaxed and calm, such as in the morning when you wake up or at night before bed. Create a personal ritual for your visualization, lighting a candle, using incense or listening to soft music, to create a conducive and inspiring environment.

Visualize in the present moment: Visualize the desired reality as if it were already a present reality, as if you were already experiencing it in the current moment. Avoid visualizing in the future, as something that "will happen one day". The subconscious responds better to images and emotions of the present moment because it interprets them as current realities.

Use affirmations in the present tense during visualization, such as "I am healthy and full of energy", "I have financial abundance and prosperity in all areas of my life", "I live loving and harmonious relationships". Feel the desired reality as if it were already yours, in the "here and now".

To help you start practicing the power of visualization, I propose the following guided visualization exercise, focused on the area of health and well-being:

Guided Visualization Exercise: Radiant Health and Vitality

Find a quiet place where you can relax without interruption for 10-15 minutes. Sit or lie down comfortably, close your eyes and take a few deep breaths to relax your body and mind.

Visualize your body radiating health and vitality. See every cell in your body glowing with vibrant energy, full of light and life. Imagine your skin luminous and healthy, your eyes bright and full of energy, your body strong and flexible.

Engage your senses in visualizing your perfect health:

Vision: See yourself practicing physical activities that you love, with ease and joy. Running, dancing, swimming, walking in nature, whatever resonates with you. See your body moving with grace, strength, and vitality.

Hearing: Hear the sound of your deep, relaxed breathing, the strong, healthy rhythm of your heart, your contagious, energetic laughter.

Touch: Feel the sensation of well-being and comfort in your body. Feel the energy vibrating in every cell, the strength in your muscles, the lightness in your movements.

Taste: Savor healthy and nutritious foods that nourish your body and give you energy and vitality. Fresh fruits, tasty vegetables, pure and invigorating water.

Smell: Smell the fresh, invigorating scent of fresh air entering your lungs, the fragrance of nature's flowers, the healthy smell of your clean, energized body.

Feel the positive emotions associated with your perfect health and well-being: joy, gratitude, vitality, energy, confidence, inner peace. Allow these emotions to fill your being, to expand beyond your body, radiating out into your entire reality.

Repeat positive affirmations about your health and well-being during visualization: "I am healthy and full of energy", "My body is strong, healthy and vibrant", "I love and care for my body with gratitude and respect", "I deserve perfect health and well-being on all levels".

Thank the universe in advance for your radiant health and vitality, as if it were already a present reality. Feel gratitude filling your heart and expanding into your reality.

Remain in this state of visualization and positive emotion for 5-10 minutes, enjoying the feeling of perfect health and well-being. When you feel ready, open your eyes and return to the present moment, taking with you the vibrant energy of your visualization.

Relax your body and mind before you start visualizing. Use deep breathing techniques, meditation or muscle relaxation to calm the mind and release body tension.

Start with short visualization sessions and gradually increase the duration as you feel more comfortable and confident.

Be patient and persistent. Visualization is a skill that develops with practice. Do not be discouraged if you do not see immediate results. Continue to practice regularly, with faith and persistence, and the results will begin to manifest in your reality.

Believe in your power to visualize and manifest. Your belief is an essential ingredient for successful visualization. Trust in your ability to create the desired reality through your mental projection.

The power of visualization is an extraordinary tool for conscious co-creation. By painting the desired reality on the canvas of your mind, with all your senses and emotions, you strengthen your mental projection, program your subconscious for success, and accelerate the manifestation process. Start practicing visualization regularly, in different areas of your life, and prepare to witness the transformative power of this art in co-creating the reality of your dreams. Paint your desired reality with vibrant colors and radiant emotions, and watch the magic of projection manifest in your life!

Chapter 13
Declaring Your New Reality

Declaring your new reality is a powerful act of conscious co-creation. When positive affirmations are repeated with conviction and emotion, they become seeds planted in the subconscious, replacing limiting beliefs with new mental programming aligned with your desires. Like a decree issued with authority, each affirmation directs your energy and strengthens your vibrational field, allowing reality to mold itself according to this new frequency. By transforming words into firm declarations, you pave the way for a clearer manifestation, accelerating the process of materializing your dreams.

Affirmations are positive statements, formulated in the present tense, that express the reality you wish to co-create. They are concise and powerful phrases that you repeat regularly, with conviction and faith, to reprogram your subconscious mind with empowering beliefs and direct your energy towards the manifestation of your desires. Affirmations are like decrees that you issue to the universe, declaring your intention to live a new reality and inviting it to manifest itself in your experience.

If thoughts and beliefs are the language of projection, and visualization is the grammar and syntax, then affirmations are the voice and pronunciation of that language. Affirmations give sound, rhythm, and vocal intention to your mental projection, making it more audible, more resonant, and more impactful to the universe. It is like transforming a silent thought into a bold and confident declaration that echoes in reality and invites it to respond.

Affirmations work because the constant repetition of positive statements programs the subconscious mind. The subconscious is like the mind's "hard drive," where our beliefs, habits, and automatic thought patterns are stored. By repeating positive affirmations consistently, we are rewriting the subconscious programming, replacing limiting beliefs with empowering beliefs, negative patterns with positive patterns, and expectations of scarcity with expectations of abundance.

The repetition of affirmations creates new neural pathways in the brain, strengthening synaptic connections associated with empowering beliefs and weakening connections associated with limiting beliefs. With time and practice, affirmations become internalized beliefs, deep convictions that manifest in your external reality.

Affirmations also direct your focus and attention. What you focus your attention on expands in your reality. By repeating positive affirmations about the areas of your life you want to improve, you are directing your focus to solutions, possibilities, and positive potential, instead of focusing on problems, limitations, and obstacles. This positive focus attracts experiences, opportunities, and resources that align with your affirmations into your life.

Furthermore, affirmations raise your energetic vibration. Words carry energy and vibration. Positive affirmations, formulated with emotion and conviction, emit a high energetic vibration that resonates with the frequency of abundance, joy, health, and success. This high vibration attracts experiences and people who vibrate at the same frequency, creating a virtuous cycle of positive manifestation.

For affirmations to be truly effective in conscious co-creation, it is important to follow some principles and guidelines:

Formulate affirmations in the present tense: Always use the present tense when formulating your affirmations, as if the desired reality were already a current reality. Avoid the future or conditional tense, such as "I will have...", "I would like to be...", "I could have...". The present moment is the only moment of power, and the subconscious responds best to affirmations in the present tense.

Instead of saying "I will be rich," say "I am rich and abundant in all areas of my life." Instead of saying "I would like to have health," say "I have perfect health and radiant vitality." Declare your new reality as if it were already a present and palpable reality.

Use positive and affirmative language: Formulate your affirmations using positive and affirmative language, focusing on what you want to attract and manifest, not what you want to avoid or eliminate.

Avoid negative words, such as "no," "never," "without," "against," which can send confusing signals to the subconscious and even attract what you don't want.

Instead of saying "I don't want any more debt," say "I am debt-free and abundant in financial resources." Instead of saying "I don't want to get sick," say "I am healthy and full of vitality." Focus on the positive, the desirable, what you want to attract into your life.

Be specific and detailed (but flexible): In some areas of life, it may be helpful to formulate specific and detailed affirmations, including sensory, emotional, and contextual details, to make your projection more vivid and directed. For example, if you want to attract a loving relationship, you can affirm: "I am in a loving, passionate, and harmonious relationship with a compatible partner who loves me, values me, and supports me in all aspects of life."

However, in other areas, it may be more beneficial to keep affirmations more generic and flexible, allowing the universe to manifest your intention in the most appropriate and surprising way. For example, if you want to attract more financial abundance, you can affirm: "I am a magnet for abundance and financial prosperity, and the universe is always providing for my needs and desires in surprising and creative ways." Trust the wisdom of the universe and leave room for divine manifestation.

Use short and memorable affirmations: Formulate your affirmations in a short, concise, and memorable way, so that it is easy to repeat and internalize them. Long and complex sentences can be difficult to memorize and maintain focus. Choose powerful and impactful words that resonate with your intention and are easy to repeat mentally or aloud.

Repeat affirmations regularly and consistently: Repetition is the key to subconscious programming. Repeat your affirmations daily, ideally several times a day, for at least 5-10 minutes per session. Consistency is more important than the duration of the sessions. It is better to repeat your affirmations for a few minutes every day than for long periods sporadically.

Set specific times for your affirmation practice: in the morning when you wake up, at night before bed, during your commute, during exercise, or whenever you feel the need to reinforce your mental projection. Create a personal ritual for your affirmation practice, combining them with visualization, conscious breathing, or inspiring music to make the experience more enjoyable and powerful.

Feel the emotion of the affirmations: Don't just repeat your affirmations like empty words, mechanically and automatically. Feel the emotion of your affirmations, connect with the feeling of already possessing, already being, or already experiencing the reality you are declaring. Feel the joy, gratitude, enthusiasm, confidence, love, peace associated with your affirmation.

Emotion is the catalyst for manifestation. Affirmations charged with positive emotion have a much greater power of subconscious programming and projection than affirmations repeated without feeling.

Engage your heart in your affirmations and let emotions amplify your power of co-creation.

Examples of powerful affirmations for various areas of life:

Health and Well-being:

"I have perfect health and radiant vitality."

"My body is strong, healthy, and full of energy."

"I love and care for my body with gratitude and respect."

"I deserve full health and well-being on all levels."

Prosperity and Abundance:

"I am a magnet for abundance and financial prosperity."

"Abundance flows easily and abundantly into my life."

"I am prosperous and abundant in all areas of my life."

"I deserve to live a rich, prosperous life full of abundance."

Loving Relationships:

"I attract loving, harmonious, and meaningful relationships into my life."

"I am loved and accepted unconditionally."

"I give and receive love in abundance, easily and naturally."

"I deserve a loving, happy, and lasting relationship."

Purpose and Fulfillment:

"I live my life's purpose with passion, joy, and fulfillment."

"I am talented, creative, and capable of achieving my dreams."

"I follow my intuition and trust my life path."

"I deserve to live a life full of meaning, purpose, and fulfillment."

Inner Peace and Happiness:

"I feel deep inner peace and serenity at all times."

"I am grateful for my life and the blessings that surround me."

"I choose to be happy and live with joy and enthusiasm every day."

"I deserve to live a life full of peace, happiness, and contentment."

To start using the power of affirmations in your conscious co-creation, do the following practical exercise:

Exercise: Creating and Practicing Powerful Affirmations

Choose an area of your life where you want to manifest positive change (health, prosperity, relationships, purpose, etc.).

Identify a limiting belief you may have in that area of life that is sabotaging your manifestation. (Review Chapter 10, if necessary).

Create one or more positive affirmations that contradict that limiting belief and that declare the reality you want to co-create in that area of life, following the principles we explored in this chapter.

Write your affirmations clearly and concisely on paper or in a journal.

Choose a specific time of day to practice your affirmations, for at least 5-10 minutes.

Relax your body and mind, take a few deep breaths, and focus on the present moment.

Repeat your affirmations aloud or mentally, with conviction, faith, and positive emotion. Feel the energy of the words vibrating in every cell of your body.

Visualize yourself living the reality declared in your affirmations, with all your senses and emotions. Combine the repetition of affirmations with visualization to strengthen your mental projection.

Practice your affirmations daily, with persistence and dedication. Consistency is the key to subconscious programming and to the manifestation of your new reality.

Adjust and refine your affirmations as needed, as your awareness expands and your desires become clearer. Affirmations are dynamic tools that can be adapted and customized to your specific needs and intentions.

The power of affirmations is an extraordinary tool for conscious co-creation. By declaring your new reality with positive words, formulated in the present and charged with emotion, you reprogram your subconscious, direct your energy, and accelerate the process of manifesting your dreams. Start using the power of affirmations daily, in all areas of your life, and prepare to witness the transformation of your reality as you declare and live the life of your dreams!

Chapter 14
Attracting Abundance and Joy

Gratitude is the key that unlocks the natural flow of abundance and joy. When we cultivate the habit of recognizing and valuing the blessings present in our lives, we adjust our vibration to attract even more reasons to be grateful. Instead of focusing on what is missing, we begin to perceive the richness around us, amplifying the feeling of contentment and fulfillment. This state of sincere appreciation not only transforms our perspective but also strengthens the connection with the universe, creating a continuous cycle of prosperity and well-being.

Gratitude is a powerful emotion of appreciation, recognition, and contentment for the blessings of life. It is the ability to value and appreciate what we already have, instead of focusing on what is missing or what we want to achieve. Gratitude is not just a fleeting feeling, but a mental attitude, a state of being that can be cultivated and practiced consciously, transforming our perspective on life and our ability to co-create the desired reality.

If thoughts and beliefs are the language of projection, visualization is the grammar, and affirmations are the voice, then gratitude is the emotion that energizes and propels that language towards manifestation. Gratitude is like the high-octane fuel that powers the engine of conscious co-creation, accelerating the manifestation process and making it smoother, more fluid, and more joyful. It is the emotion that transforms intention into reality, desire into experience, projection into manifestation.

How does the power of gratitude work?

Gratitude works on multiple levels, influencing your inner and outer reality in a profound and transformative way:

Raises your energetic vibration: Gratitude is an emotion of high vibrational frequency, which resonates with the energy of abundance, joy, love, and positivity. By cultivating gratitude, you raise your personal energetic vibration, tuning into the frequency of the reality you want to co-create. The law of attraction states that like attracts like, and by vibrating at the frequency of gratitude, you attract experiences, people, and opportunities that resonate with that same high frequency into your life.

Shifts your focus to the positive: The practice of gratitude shifts your focus from lack to abundance, from negativity to positivity, from problems to solutions. Instead of focusing on what you don't have, what isn't working, or what makes you unhappy, gratitude invites you to recognize and appreciate the blessings that are already present in your life, no matter how small or insignificant they may seem. This positive focus expands your perception, opens your eyes to the opportunities and resources available, and attracts more reasons to be grateful in your reality.

Opens the flow of abundance: Gratitude is like a key that opens the door to the flow of abundance in all areas of your life. By appreciating what you already have, you send a message to the universe that you are open and receptive to abundance, that you value the blessings you receive, and that you are ready to receive even more. The universe responds to this sign of gratitude by sending more blessings, more opportunities, and more abundance into your life, in a virtuous cycle of giving and receiving.

- Amplifies joy and contentment: Gratitude increases your sense of joy and contentment with life. By appreciating the present moment and the blessings that surround you, you free yourself from the incessant search for something "more" or "better" in the future, and begin to savor and enjoy the beauty and abundance that already exist in your current reality. Gratitude transforms your perspective, making the ordinary extraordinary, the simple valuable, the everyday magical.

Strengthens relationships: Gratitude strengthens your relationships with others. Expressing gratitude to the people in your life nurtures bonds of affection, strengthens emotional connection, and creates an environment of harmony and mutual appreciation. Gratitude in relationships generates reciprocity, kindness, and generosity, creating virtuous circles of love and support.

How to practice gratitude consciously:

Cultivating gratitude as a daily and conscious practice is a simple but profoundly transformative process. Here are some practical techniques and suggestions to integrate gratitude into your daily life:

Gratitude Journal: Set aside a few minutes each day, preferably in the morning when you wake up or at night before bed, to write in a gratitude journal. Write down 3 to 5 things you are grateful for that day, or in your life in general. They can be big or small things, material or immaterial, everyday or special. The important thing is to recognize and appreciate the blessings that surround you.

Examples of things you can be grateful for: your health, your family, your friends, your home, your work, nature, food, water, the sun, your ability to love, learn, create, etc. Vary your gratitude list every day, always looking for new reasons to be grateful.

Gratitude List: If you prefer, instead of writing a journal, you can create a mental gratitude list before bed or upon waking. Think of several things you are grateful for and savor the emotion of gratitude for each item on the list. The simple act of consciously thinking about things you are grateful for already raises your vibration and opens the flow of abundance.

Gratitude Walk: Turn your daily walks into a gratitude practice. As you walk, observe the world around you and find reasons to be grateful in every detail: the beauty of nature, the air you breathe, the sun warming your skin, the sounds of the city, the people passing by, etc. Feel gratitude filling your heart as you walk and appreciate the blessings that surround you.

Gratitude Affirmations: Incorporate gratitude affirmations into your daily affirmation practice. Create affirmations that express your gratitude for the blessings you already have, and for the blessings that are coming into your life. Examples of gratitude affirmations: "I am grateful for all the blessings in my life," "I give thanks for the abundance that constantly flows to me," "I recognize and appreciate the beauty and magic of my life," "I am grateful for having everything I need and desire." Repeat these affirmations with emotion and conviction to strengthen your gratitude practice.

Gratitude Letters: Write gratitude letters to important people in your life, expressing your appreciation and recognition for the positive impact they have on you. Send these letters (or deliver them personally, if possible) to strengthen your relationships and radiate gratitude to the world. Writing gratitude letters is a powerful practice to nurture emotional bonds and express your love and recognition to the people around you.

Gratitude Visualization: Combine your visualization practice with the emotion of gratitude. As you visualize the desired reality, feel deep gratitude for already experiencing it, as if it were already a present reality. Gratitude amplifies the power of visualization and accelerates the manifestation process.

Daily Act of Gratitude: Choose a conscious act of gratitude to practice every day. It can be something simple like verbally thanking someone, giving a sincere compliment, offering help to someone, making a donation, sending a message of appreciation, etc. Small acts of gratitude radiate positive energy to the world and strengthen your mental attitude of gratitude.

Tips for cultivating gratitude:

Start small and be consistent: You don't have to transform your life overnight. Start with small gratitude practices and be consistent in your daily practice. Consistency is more important than initial intensity.

Look for gratitude in all situations: Challenge yourself to find reasons to be grateful even in challenging or negative situations. Even in difficult times, there are always blessings in disguise or lessons to be learned. Gratitude transforms your perspective and helps you find the positive in all situations.

Be specific in your gratitude: Instead of giving thanks in a generic way, be specific about what you are grateful for and why. Instead of saying "I am grateful for my health," say "I am grateful for my vibrant energy and my body's ability to heal and function perfectly." Specificity makes gratitude more heartfelt and powerful.

Feel the emotion of gratitude: Don't just practice gratitude mentally or superficially. Feel the emotion of gratitude in your heart, let it fill your being, savor the feeling of appreciation and contentment. Emotion is what gives life and power to your gratitude practice.

Share your gratitude: Expressing your gratitude to others amplifies your experience of gratitude and strengthens your relationships. Share your gratitude with the people you love, with your friends, with your family, with your colleagues, with the universe. Radiate gratitude to the world and see it return multiplied to your life.

The power of gratitude is immense and transformative. By cultivating gratitude as a daily and conscious practice, you raise your energetic vibration, open the flow of abundance, amplify your joy and contentment, strengthen your relationships, and accelerate the process of conscious co-creation. Start practicing gratitude today, in all areas of your life, and prepare to attract an abundant, joyful, and blessed reality. Open your heart to gratitude and see the magic manifest in your life!

Chapter 15
Amplifying Your Projection

Positive emotions are the driving force that enhances the manifestation of your desired reality. More than just fleeting feelings, they function as high vibrational frequencies that amplify mental projection, attracting experiences aligned with this energy. When we cultivate emotional states like joy, gratitude, and enthusiasm, we strengthen our faith in co-creation and awaken a magnetic field that resonates with abundance and fulfillment. This emotional attunement transforms not only our perception of the present but also accelerates the realization of our desires, making the manifestation process more fluid and natural.

Positive emotions, such as joy, love, enthusiasm, gratitude, hope, trust, compassion, and peace, are not just pleasant states of mind or "good feelings." They are vibrant energy forces, powerful catalysts of conscious co-creation, that act as amplifiers of your intention, propelling your mental projection with unparalleled energy. Positive emotions are the "turbocharged combustion" of the engine of manifestation, the secret ingredient that transforms potential into reality, desire into tangible experience.

If thoughts and beliefs are the language, visualization the grammar, affirmations the voice, and gratitude the fuel, then positive emotions are the electricity that lights the lamp of conscious projection, illuminating the path of manifestation and radiating your intention to the universe with an irresistible force. Positive emotions are the very essence of life force, creative energy in motion, the vibrant dance of consciousness manifesting itself in reality.

How Positive Emotions Amplify Your Projection

Positive emotions act as amplifiers of your mental projection through several interconnected mechanisms:

Increase your vibrational frequency: As mentioned in the previous chapter, positive emotions vibrate at a higher energetic frequency than negative emotions like fear, anger, sadness, or guilt. By cultivating positive emotions, you raise your overall vibrational frequency, attuning yourself to the frequency of abundance, joy, health, and success. This high vibration attracts experiences that resonate with that same frequency, like a magnet attracting iron filings.

Strengthen your belief and faith: Positive emotions strengthen your belief in the possibility of manifestation and your faith in the process of conscious co-creation. When you feel joyful, enthusiastic, and confident, your subconscious mind becomes more receptive to your intentions and desires, dispelling doubts and inner resistance. Positive emotions act as a powerful mental "placebo," convincing your subconscious that the desired reality is real, possible, and on its way to materializing.

Direct your focus to potential and opportunities: Positive emotions expand your perception and open your eyes to the potential and opportunities that surround you. When you feel optimistic and hopeful, you become more receptive to new ideas, creative solutions, synchronicities, and meaningful "coincidences" that can drive the manifestation of your desires. Positive emotions act as a mental "radar," guiding you to the paths, people, and situations that align with your intention.

Increase your energy and motivation: Positive emotions energize your body and mind, increasing your motivation to act towards your goals and overcome challenges that may arise on the path of manifestation. When you feel inspired and enthusiastic, you become more proactive, resilient, and persistent in pursuing your dreams. Positive emotions act as an energy "boost," propelling you to act with confidence and determination.

Create a magnetic field of attraction: Positive emotions radiate outward, creating a magnetic field of attraction that draws into your life people, situations, and resources that align with your vibration and intentions. Positive emotions act as an energetic "beacon," emitting a clear signal to the universe that you are open and receptive to abundance, joy, and love. The universe responds to this signal by sending you what you are radiating, in a continuous positive feedback loop.

How to Cultivate and Amplify Positive Emotions

Cultivating and amplifying positive emotions in your daily life is an ongoing and intentional process that involves various practices and approaches:

Conscious Gratitude Practices: As explored in the previous chapter, the daily practice of gratitude is one of the most effective ways to cultivate and amplify positive emotions. Take moments throughout your day to acknowledge and appreciate the blessings in your life, big and small, and feel the emotion of gratitude fill your heart.

Meditation and Mindfulness: Meditation and mindfulness are powerful tools to calm the mind, reduce stress and anxiety, and open space for positive emotions to flourish. Practice meditation regularly, focusing on your breath, bodily sensations, or guided visualizations that evoke positive emotions like love, compassion, and joy.

Enjoyable and Inspiring Activities: Regularly dedicate time to activities that bring you pleasure, joy, and inspiration. These can be creative hobbies, activities in nature, moments of socializing with loved ones, artistic practices, sports, inspirational reading, listening to uplifting music, etc. Invest time and energy in activities that nourish your soul and evoke positive emotions in your being.

Positive Affirmations and Visualizations: Use positive affirmations and visualizations to program your subconscious mind with empowering emotions. Combine your affirmations and visualizations with the genuine emotion of joy, love, gratitude, and enthusiasm.

Feel the positive emotions filling your being as you repeat the affirmations and visualize the desired reality.

Surround Yourself with Positivity: Cultivate positive relationships with people who support, inspire, and uplift you. Seek the company of people who radiate joy, optimism, and enthusiasm for life. Reduce or eliminate contact with negative, toxic, or pessimistic people who drain your energy and undermine your positive emotions. Create a positive environment around you, surrounding yourself with beauty, harmony, cheerful colors, inspiring music, and sensory stimuli that evoke positive emotions.

Practice Self-Compassion and Self-Love: Treat yourself with kindness, compassion, and unconditional love. Forgive yourself for your mistakes, accept your imperfections, and celebrate your qualities and achievements. Cultivate a positive and encouraging inner dialogue, and nurture your self-esteem and self-confidence. Self-love is the foundation for all other positive emotions to flourish in your life.

Daily Act of Kindness: Practice acts of kindness and generosity towards others daily. Helping others, making someone smile, offering a gesture of affection, practicing compassion and empathy are powerful ways to generate positive emotions in yourself and others, creating a virtuous cycle of kindness and joy.

Integrating Positive Emotions into Your Co-creation

To integrate the power of positive emotions into your conscious co-creation practice, try the following practical strategies:

Start each day with gratitude and joy: Upon waking, before starting your day, take a few minutes to feel gratitude for the blessings in your life and to evoke emotions of joy and enthusiasm for the day ahead. This morning practice sets the emotional tone for the entire day and prepares your mind and heart to attract positive experiences.

Visualize and affirm with emotion: When practicing visualization and affirmations, consciously engage your positive emotions. Feel joy, gratitude, enthusiasm, love, and confidence as you visualize your desired reality and repeat your affirmations. Let emotions amplify the power of your mental projection and your intention to manifest.

Use emotion as a guide: Pay attention to your emotions throughout the day as an indicator of your alignment with your conscious co-creation. Positive emotions indicate that you are vibrating at the frequency of your desired reality and attracting positive experiences. Negative emotions signal misalignment and an invitation to reorient your thoughts, beliefs, and intentions, and to cultivate more positive emotions.

Celebrate small victories and progress: Throughout the co-creation process, celebrate small victories, incremental progress, and synchronicities that appear in your life as signs that your projection is working and that your desired reality is on its way to manifesting. Celebration strengthens your faith, increases your motivation, and amplifies your positive emotions, further accelerating the co-creation process.

The power of positive emotions is a transformative force in conscious co-creation. By cultivating and amplifying positive emotions in your daily life, you raise your energetic vibration, strengthen your belief, direct your focus, increase your energy, and create a magnetic field of attraction for your desired reality. Start integrating the power of positive emotions into your co-creation practice today, and prepare to witness an extraordinary amplification of your ability to manifest the life of your dreams, with joy, fluidity, and abundance!

Chapter 16
Overcoming Resistance

The path of conscious co-creation demands more than knowledge and intention; it demands overcoming the internal barriers that inevitably arise along the journey. Facing resistance does not mean failure, but rather an invitation to growth and transformation. It is at this point that the true strength of the co-creator is revealed: by recognizing and understanding internal challenges, it becomes possible to dissolve the limitations imposed by ingrained beliefs, fears, and conditioned patterns. Thus, each obstacle transforms into a step towards evolution, strengthening the connection with one's own creative power and leading to a more aligned and conscious manifestation of the desired reality.

Resistance in conscious co-creation manifests itself in various forms, such as doubts, fears, persistent limiting beliefs, unconscious sabotage, lack of patience, discouragement, or the feeling that "it's not working." This resistance is not a sign of failure or that conscious co-creation is not real, but rather a natural process of growth and transformation. Resistance is like the friction we feel when moving a heavy object: it requires more effort, but it also strengthens our muscles and increases our ability to overcome.

Resistance arises because conscious co-creation implies a profound paradigm shift, a transformation in our way of thinking, feeling, and acting in the world. We are unlearning patterns of thought and behavior conditioned by fear, limitation, and passivity, and relearning to live from a place of power, intention, and awareness. This transition is not always easy or immediate, and it is natural to encounter resistance along the way.

It is essential to understand the nature of resistance in order to overcome it effectively. Resistance can have several origins:

Deeply rooted limiting beliefs: Even after the work of releasing limiting beliefs that we explored in Chapter 10, some negative beliefs can remain rooted in the subconscious, exerting a subtle but persistent influence on our mental projection. These beliefs can generate doubts, fears, and unconscious sabotage, undermining our conscious co-creation efforts.

Past programming and Collective Consciousness: We have been conditioned since childhood to believe in a limited reality based on scarcity, struggle, and powerlessness. The influence of the Collective Consciousness, with its dominant and limiting beliefs, can also generate resistance to shifting to a reality of abundance, ease, and personal power.

Fear of change and the unknown: Conscious co-creation invites us to step out of our comfort zone, to abandon the familiar and known, and to venture into new and unknown territory where we are the authors of our own reality. This process can generate fear, anxiety, and insecurity, especially at the beginning when the results of conscious co-creation are not yet fully visible.

Lack of patience and unrealistic expectations: The manifestation of the desired reality through conscious co-creation does not always happen instantly or immediately. It requires time, persistence, practice, and above all, patience. Lack of patience and unrealistic expectations of quick results can lead to discouragement, frustration, and premature abandonment of the practice of conscious co-creation.

Tests from the Universe and growth challenges: Sometimes, the challenges and obstacles we encounter on the path of conscious co-creation can be tests from the universe to assess our determination, our faith, and our alignment with our intention. These challenges can also be opportunities for personal growth, developing resilience, overcoming limitations, and expanding our consciousness.

Strategies to Overcome Resistance and Navigate Challenges

Overcoming resistance and navigating the challenges of conscious co-creation requires awareness, strategy, perseverance, and above all, self-compassion. Here are some practical and effective strategies:

Recognize and accept resistance as natural: The first step is to recognize and accept resistance as a normal and natural part of the conscious co-creation process. Don't criticize or judge yourself for feeling resistance. Instead, see resistance as a sign that you are challenging your limits, expanding your awareness, and growing beyond your comfort zone. Resistance is an indicator that you are on the right track, transforming your reality.

Identify the source of the resistance: Seek to identify the underlying causes of your resistance. Ask yourself: "What is the fear or doubt behind this resistance? What limiting belief is being activated? What negative thought pattern is sabotaging my projection?" By understanding the source of the resistance, you can address it more consciously and effectively.

Reaffirm your commitment to conscious co-creation: When resistance arises, reinforce your commitment to conscious co-creation by reminding yourself of your authentic desires, your deepest values, and your life purpose. Reread your written intentions, review your visualizations, repeat your affirmations, and reconnect with your initial motivation for embarking on this transformative journey. Reaffirm your power as an Inner Projector and your determination to co-create the reality of your dreams.

Transform persistent limiting beliefs: If you identify persistent limiting beliefs behind your resistance, reinforce the work of releasing limiting beliefs that we explored in Chapter 10. Use the techniques of logical questioning, reframing experience, searching for exceptions, and replacing with empowering beliefs to dismantle and transform these negative beliefs. Persistence in transforming limiting beliefs is essential to overcome resistance and pave the way for manifestation.

Cultivate patience and persistence: Remember that conscious co-creation is a gradual process, not an instant event. Cultivate patience with yourself and with the rhythm of the universe. Trust that your desired reality is manifesting in perfect timing and in the most appropriate way. Persist in your practice of visualization, affirmations, gratitude, and positive emotions, even when results are not immediately visible. Persistence is the key to breaking through resistance and reaping the fruits of conscious co-creation.

Celebrate small progress and synchronicities: Instead of focusing on what has not yet manifested, celebrate the small steps forward, synchronicities, and small victories that arise along the way. Recognize and appreciate each sign that your projection is working, each meaningful "coincidence," each unexpected opportunity, each small improvement in your reality. Celebration strengthens your faith, increases your motivation, and amplifies positive emotions, creating a virtuous cycle of manifestation.

Seek support and inspiration: When you feel discouraged or overwhelmed by resistance, seek support and inspiration from external sources. Talk to friends or mentors who understand the journey of conscious co-creation, participate in online or in-person support groups, read inspiring books, listen to motivational podcasts, or watch uplifting videos. External support and inspiration can give you the extra boost of energy and motivation to overcome resistance and keep moving forward.

Reframe challenges as growth opportunities: Instead of viewing challenges and obstacles as signs of failure or that conscious co-creation "doesn't work," reframe them as opportunities for personal growth and strengthening your co-creative abilities. Ask yourself: "What can I learn from this challenge? How can I use this situation to expand my awareness and strengthen my faith? What new qualities and abilities can I develop by overcoming this obstacle?" Reframing challenges transforms resistance into a springboard for your growth and the manifestation of your desired reality.

Practice self-compassion and kindness: Be kind and compassionate to yourself as you navigate the resistance and challenges of conscious co-creation. Don't put excessive pressure on yourself, don't criticize yourself for your mistakes or doubts, and don't compare yourself to others. Treat yourself with the same understanding, patience, and love that you would offer a dear friend who is going through a difficult time. Self-compassion and kindness strengthen your resilience and your ability to overcome resistance with lightness and balance.

Resistance is an inevitable part of the journey of conscious co-creation, but it doesn't have to be an insurmountable obstacle. By understanding the nature of resistance, using effective strategies to overcome it, and cultivating patience, persistence, and self-compassion, you can navigate challenges with confidence and determination, transforming resistance into a springboard for your personal growth and the manifestation of the reality of your dreams. Remember that resistance is a sign that you are moving forward, expanding your consciousness, and co-creating a life increasingly aligned with your unlimited potential. Embrace resistance as part of the journey, and keep dancing with conscious projection, overcoming all challenges with grace and power!

Chapter 17
Flowing with the Universe and Releasing Control

The journey of conscious co-creation reaches a new level when we recognize that true power lies not only in directing reality with intention and focus, but also in allowing the universe to act with its infinite intelligence. The balance between action and surrender proves to be essential, for when we trust in the flow of life and release the need for control, we open space for manifestations to occur in the highest and most harmonious way. This process does not mean passivity, but rather an active and conscious collaboration with greater forces, where the synergy between desire and trust allows for a more fluid, natural, and expansive creation.

Conscious co-creation is not just about imposing our will on the universe, shaping reality in our image and likeness. It is also about collaborating with the infinite intelligence of the universe, trusting in the flow of life, and allowing divine wisdom to guide us beyond our limited plans. It is about finding the perfect balance between focused intention and trusting surrender, between conscious effort and graceful letting go.

The need for control is an illusion of the egoic mind, an attempt to grasp and manipulate reality to feel safe and secure. Excessive control, paradoxically, generates resistance, tension, and anxiety, blocking the natural flow of abundance and joy. When we try to control every detail of the manifestation process, we close ourselves off to spontaneity, creativity, and the wonderful surprises that the universe has to offer us.

True conscious co-creation flourishes when we learn to dance with surrender, when we trust that the universe is conspiring in our favor, even when the path ahead is not clear or when the results do not exactly match our initial expectations. Surrender is not passivity or resignation, but rather a state of active receptivity, deep trust, and openness to the flow of life. It is the wisdom of planting the seeds of intention with focus and clarity, and then letting the universe nurture them and make them bloom at the perfect time and in the most appropriate way.

The Paradoxes of Intention and Surrender

It may seem paradoxical to speak of focused intention and trusting surrender in the same sentence. Aren't they opposing concepts? How is it possible to be simultaneously intentional and surrendered? It is precisely in this paradox that lies the key to mastering conscious co-creation.

Intention is the compass that directs our creative energy, the beacon that illuminates the path of manifestation, the seed that we plant with clarity and purpose. Surrender is the water that nourishes the seed, the sun that warms it, the earth that sustains it, the wind that spreads its petals, allowing it to grow and flourish naturally and organically, beyond our limited control.

Intention without surrender can become rigidity, obsession, and excessive control, generating tension, anxiety, and resistance. Surrender without intention can become passivity, inertia, and lack of direction, resulting in frustration, discouragement, and lack of fulfillment. The dance of conscious co-creation is finding the dynamic balance between these two poles, integrating the strength of focused intention with the lightness of trusting surrender.

Principles of the Dance of Surrender

To dance with surrender in conscious co-creation, we can cultivate some key principles:

Trust in the Universe and Infinite Intelligence: The fundamental principle of surrender is deep trust in the universe, in the infinite intelligence that governs creation, in the divine wisdom that guides the flow of life. Trust that the universe is benevolent, abundant, and always conspiring in your favor, even when appearances suggest otherwise. Trust that there is a greater plan in action, beyond your limited understanding, and that this plan is working for your highest good, even when the path becomes winding or challenging.

Release of Excessive Control and Attachment to Outcome: Learn to release excessive control over the manifestation process and obsessive attachment to the specific outcome. Define your intentions with clarity and focus, visualize the desired reality with emotion and conviction, repeat your affirmations with faith and persistence, but then surrender the outcome to the universe, trusting that it will manifest at the perfect time and in the most appropriate way. Detach from the need to control how, when, and where your intention will manifest, and open yourself to the possibility of the universe surprising you with solutions and paths even better than those you could imagine.

Acceptance of the Present Moment and the Flow of Life: Surrender implies accepting the present moment as it is, without resistance, without judgment, without regrets about the past or anxiety about the future. Accept current circumstances as a starting point, as a step in your conscious co-creation journey, and trust that the universe is guiding you to the next step on the path of manifestation. Flow with the natural rhythm of life, with its ups and downs, with its cycles of creation and destruction, with its constant dance of change and transformation.

Listening to Intuition and Following Inner Guidance: Surrender opens space to listen to your intuition and follow the inner guidance that the universe sends you through signs, synchronicities, dreams, insights, and inspirations. Be attentive to the whispers of your soul, the messages of your heart, the creative impulses that arise spontaneously in your mind. Trust your inner wisdom and follow the divine guidance that guides you to the path of manifestation most aligned with your purpose and your highest good.

Gratitude for the Process and not Just the Outcome: Cultivate gratitude not only for the final outcome of the manifestation, but also for the process itself. Appreciate each step of the journey, each challenge overcome, each lesson learned, each small victory celebrated. Recognize the beauty and magic of each present moment, even when the path seems uncertain or difficult. Gratitude for the process strengthens your faith, fuels your perseverance, and makes the journey of conscious co-creation more enjoyable and meaningful.

Surrender to the Divine Flow and the Higher Will: The deepest surrender implies surrendering to the divine flow, to the higher will of the One Consciousness, recognizing that you are just an instrument in the cosmic dance of creation. Surrender your desires and intentions to a force greater than yourself, trusting that divine wisdom will guide you beyond your limited plans, to a higher and more meaningful destiny than you could imagine. This surrender is not an abdication of your personal power, but rather its highest expression, the conscious collaboration with the infinite intelligence of the universe for the manifestation of the greatest good for you and for all creation.

Practicing Surrender in Conscious Co-creation

To integrate the dance of surrender into your conscious co-creation practice, try the following practical suggestions:

Surrender Meditation: Set aside daily time for surrender meditation. Sit in silence, breathe deeply, and imagine yourself surrendering your desires and intentions to the universe, as if you were depositing seeds in a fertile garden and trusting that they will bloom at the perfect time. Visualize yourself releasing control, letting go of attachment to the outcome, and opening yourself to divine wisdom and guidance. Feel the peace, confidence, and serenity of surrender filling your being.

Affirmations of Surrender: Incorporate affirmations of surrender into your daily practice. Examples of surrender affirmations: "I trust the flow of the universe and surrender my desires to divine wisdom", "I release control and allow the universe to manifest my dreams in the best possible way", "I trust the guidance of my intuition and follow the flow of life with serenity and confidence", "I accept the present moment with gratitude and open myself to the wonderful surprises that the universe has for me". Repeat these affirmations with conviction and faith, to reprogram your subconscious mind with the attitude of surrender.

Visualization of Surrender: Combine your visualization practice with the image of surrender. Visualize yourself surrendering your desires and intentions to the universe as if you were launching a paper boat into a flowing river and trusting that it will sail safely to its final destination. Visualize yourself opening your hands, letting go of control, and allowing the current of life to guide you beyond your limited expectations. Feel the lightness, freedom, and confidence of surrender enveloping your being.

Inspired Actions and Detachment from Outcome: When acting towards your goals, seek to follow your intuition and inspired impulses, rather than trying to rigidly and planned control every step of the way. Do your best in each action, with focus and dedication, but detach from the specific outcome. Trust that the universe will coordinate events, people, and circumstances in a way that aligns with your intention, even if the end result is different from what you initially imagined. Be open to the surprises and twists of fate, and trust that everything is happening for your highest good.

Acceptance of "Deviations" and "Delays" as part of the Divine Plan: When the path of manifestation becomes winding, when seemingly unwanted "deviations" or "delays" arise, seek to accept these situations as part of the divine plan, as opportunities for learning, growth, and realignment with your original intention. Instead of resisting or regretting the "detours", seek to learn from them, adapt to the new circumstances, and trust that the universe is guiding you to an even better destination than the one you initially planned. Often, "detours" and "delays" are apparent detours that lead us to a path even more aligned with our purpose and our happiness.

The dance of surrender is the art of harmonizing focused intention with unwavering trust in the universe. It is the wisdom of planting the seeds of your desires with clarity and purpose, and then letting the universe nurture them and make them bloom at the perfect time and in the most appropriate way. By learning to dance with surrender, you free yourself from the weight of excessive control, open yourself to the magic of synchronicity, and allow abundance, joy, and fulfillment to flow freely into your life. Start practicing the dance of surrender today, and discover the lightness, fluidity, and beauty of co-creating your reality in harmony with the universe!

Chapter 18
Conscious Co-creation in Motion

Conscious co-creation comes to life when we unite intention and action, allowing our desires to transform into reality through movements aligned with our essence. It is not enough to just dream, visualize, or affirm; it is necessary to act in an inspired way, following the impulses that are born from intuition and inner alignment. Each step taken with confidence and purpose becomes a link between the invisible and the tangible, opening the way for opportunities, synchronicities, and manifestations that reflect the deep connection between our consciousness and the ever-flowing universe.

Conscious co-creation is not just an internal and mental process, limited to the domain of thoughts, beliefs, and emotions. It is also a dynamic and active process, which manifests itself in the world through our actions, our choices, and our behaviors. Inspired action is the bridge that connects the inner world of intention and projection to the outer world of manifested reality. It is the movement, the flow, the dance that puts conscious co-creation into action, making it tangible and palpable in our daily lives.

Inspired action is not just any action, mechanical or automatic, motivated by fear, obligation, or external expectation. It is an action that is born from intuition, from alignment with our inner truth, from resonance with our life purpose, from the divine guidance we receive through our expanded consciousness. Inspired action is light, fluid, natural, spontaneous, and charged with enthusiasm, joy, and passion. It is an action that propels us forward with confidence, that guides us to the right opportunities, that aligns us with the people and circumstances that harmonize with our intention.

If thoughts and beliefs are the language, visualization the grammar, affirmations the voice, gratitude the fuel, positive emotions the electricity, and surrender the dance, then inspired action is the body in motion, the physical expression of conscious co-creation manifesting itself in the world. It is the materialization of intention, the realization of vision, the translation of dreams into tangible reality. Inspired action is the bridge between the invisible and the visible, between potential and manifestation, between consciousness and experience.

Characteristics of Inspired Action

Inspired action is distinguished from ordinary action by some essential characteristics:

Born from Intuition and Inner Guidance: Inspired action is not motivated by rational logic, strategic calculation, or external pressure, but by the soft and wise voice of intuition, by the inner guidance that arises from our heart, our soul, our connection with the One Consciousness. It is an action that we feel is "right", "aligned", "natural", even if the rational mind does not fully understand why. Inspired action arises from a place of inner wisdom that transcends the logical and linear mind.

Lightness, Fluidity, and Ease: Inspired action is not forced, tense, or heavy, but rather light, fluid, and easy. When we are acting inspired, we feel that we are "going with the flow", that the universe is conspiring in our favor, that doors open spontaneously, that synchronicities manifest naturally, that obstacles dissolve with ease. Inspired action feels pleasurable, rewarding, and energizing, rather than exhausting, frustrating, or discouraging.

Enthusiasm, Joy, and Passion: Inspired action is motivated by passion, enthusiasm, and joy. It is an action that makes us feel alive, excited, and fulfilled. When we are acting inspired, we feel an inner fire driving us forward, a vibrant energy that moves us with confidence and determination. Inspired action feels exciting, motivating, and inspiring, both for us and for others who are touched by our action.

Alignment with Purpose and Values: Inspired action is aligned with our life purpose and our deepest values. It is an action that contributes to our personal fulfillment, our spiritual growth, and the greater good of all involved. Inspired action feels meaningful, valuable, and purposeful, rather than empty, superficial, or selfish.

Openness to Synchronicity and Magic: Inspired action opens space for synchronicity and magic to manifest in our lives. When we are acting inspired, the universe responds with signs, coincidences, and seemingly "miraculous" events that guide us on the path of manifestation, that connect us with the right people and opportunities, that reveal unexpected and creative solutions to us. Inspired action feels magical, surprising, and full of synchronicity, as if the universe were dancing with us in perfect harmony.

How to Integrate Inspired Action into Conscious Co-creation

Integrating inspired action into your conscious co-creation practice is an ongoing process of inner listening, alignment with intuition, and spontaneous response to divine impulses. Here are some practical strategies for cultivating and following inspired action:

Cultivate Inner Listening and Intuition: The first step to inspired action is to develop the ability to listen to the voice of your intuition and trust your inner guidance. Set aside daily time to silence the rational mind, to calm the external noise, and to connect with the wisdom of your heart, through meditation, mindfulness, contemplation in nature, or other practices of introspection. Learn to distinguish the voice of intuition from the noises of the egoic mind, such as fear, doubt, anxiety, or judgment. Intuition usually manifests as a feeling of inner certainty, a silent knowing, a spontaneous impulse, a creative idea, or a feeling of resonance in the body.

Ask for Guidance and Be Receptive to Signs: Before making a decision or acting in a certain direction, ask the universe, your intuition, your higher consciousness for guidance. Formulate your question with clarity and openness, and be receptive to the signs and answers that arise in various ways: through dreams, synchronicities, conversations, books, messages, feelings, or spontaneous insights. Trust that the universe will guide you to the right path if you are willing to listen and follow divine guidance.

Act in the Present Moment and with Spontaneity: Inspired action arises in the present moment, from the spontaneous response to the flow of life, from attunement to the rhythm of the universe. Avoid excessive planning, controlling every detail, or postponing action for the future. When you feel a clear and positive impulse to act in a certain direction, move forward with confidence and spontaneity, without hesitation, without procrastination, without over-analyzing the consequences. Inspired action is agile, immediate, and aligned with the flow of the present moment.

Follow Enthusiasm and Joy as Guides: Enthusiasm and joy are signs that you are on the path of inspired action. Pay attention to the activities, people, opportunities that make you feel enthusiastic, joyful, and passionate. Follow your enthusiasm as a guide, trust your joy as a compass, and invest your time and energy in the areas of your life that resonate with your inner passion. Inspired action feels rewarding, energizing, and full of vitality.

Trust the Flow and Detach from the Outcome: When acting inspired, trust the flow of the universe and detach from the specific outcome. Do your best in each action, with dedication and excellence, but release the need to control the final outcome. Trust that the universe will coordinate events and circumstances in a way that aligns with your highest intention, even if the outcome is different from what you initially expected. Inspired action is surrendered to the divine flow, confident that the universe will provide the best possible outcome, at the perfect time and in the most appropriate way.

Observe the Signs and Synchronicities: After acting inspired, be attentive to the signs and synchronicities that arise in your life as feedback from the universe. Observe the meaningful "coincidences", the unexpected opportunities, the messages that resonate with you, the doors that open spontaneously. These signs are validations from the universe that you are on the right path, that your action is aligned with the flow of creation, that manifestation is unfolding in a harmonious and magical way. Synchronicity is the language of the universe communicating with us, guiding us and supporting us on our journey of conscious co-creation.

Integrating Inspired Action into Daily Practice

To begin integrating inspired action into your daily conscious co-creation practice, try the following practical exercises:

Meditation of Inspired Action: Set aside daily time for meditation on inspired action. Sit in silence, breathe deeply, and visualize yourself receiving intuitive guidance on the inspired actions you can take in your daily life. Ask yourself: "What are the inspired actions I can take today to bring me closer to my goals and my life purpose? What steps can I take that are light, fluid, and aligned with my joy and enthusiasm?". Be receptive to the answers that arise in your mind, your heart, and your body, and write down the ideas and impulses you receive.

Journal of Inspired Action: Keep a journal of inspired action. At the end of each day, reflect on the actions you took throughout the day and identify those that were truly inspired, that arose from intuition, enthusiasm, and spontaneity, and that brought positive results and synchronicities into your life. Write down the characteristics of the inspired action, the emotions you felt while acting, the results you achieved, and the signs of validation from the universe that you witnessed. This journal will help you refine your ability to recognize and follow inspired action.

Weekly Inspired Action Challenge: Set a weekly inspired action challenge. Choose an area of your life where you want to manifest positive change, and commit to taking at least one inspired action per day in that area, for a week. These can be small or large actions, simple or complex, the important thing is that they are actions that arise from intuition, enthusiasm, and alignment with your inner truth. Observe the results and synchronicities that arise throughout the week and celebrate the power of inspired action in your life.

Inspired Action Accountability Partner: Find an accountability partner who is also practicing conscious co-creation and integrating inspired action into their life. Share your experiences, your challenges, your achievements, and your learnings. Encourage each other to follow inspired action, overcome resistance, and celebrate progress. Support and sharing with an accountability partner can strengthen your motivation and perseverance on the journey of conscious co-creation in motion.

Inspired action is the essence of conscious co-creation in motion. By integrating inspired action into your daily practice, you transform your mental projection into tangible reality, manifesting your desires and dreams in the world in a fluid, spontaneous, and magical way. Start cultivating inner listening today, following your intuition, acting inspired by enthusiasm and joy, and dancing with the current of life towards the reality you long to co-create. Let inspired action be the moving body of your conscious co-creation, and prepare to live a life full of purpose, passion, and abundant manifestation!

Chapter 19
Co-creating Relationships

Relationships are living reflections of our energy, mirroring back what we project consciously or unconsciously. Each interaction is an opportunity to create more authentic and harmonious connections, transforming bonds into sources of growth and mutual fulfillment. By bringing awareness to how we relate, we can intentionally cultivate love, respect, and understanding, shaping our interpersonal experiences in a lighter and more meaningful way. Thus, we become active co-creators of relationships that nurture, inspire, and elevate our journey.

Relationships are the theater of our human experience, the stage where much of our life journey unfolds, where we learn, grow, love, suffer, and evolve. Relationships can be sources of deep joy, support, connection, and fulfillment, but they can also be scenarios of conflict, pain, frustration, and misunderstanding. The quality of our relationships profoundly influences our well-being, our happiness, and our ability to co-create a full and meaningful life.

The good news is that the principles of conscious co-creation also apply to relationships. Just as we co-create our individual reality through our thoughts, beliefs, intentions, and emotions, we also co-create the dynamics and quality of our relationships through our mental projections, our expectations, our attitudes, and our behaviors. By understanding the mechanisms of conscious co-creation in relationships, we can become more skillful and conscious co-creators of harmonious, loving, and enriching interactions.

Projection in Relationships: The Mirror Effect

In relationships, the principle of projection manifests itself in a particularly evident way through the "mirror effect". What we project into our relationships, consciously or unconsciously, tends to be reflected back to us through the behavior, attitudes, and reactions of other people. If we project love, trust, respect, and understanding, we are more likely to receive love, trust, respect, and understanding in return. If, on the other hand, we project fear, distrust, judgment, and criticism, we are more likely to receive fear, distrust, judgment, and criticism in return.

This mirror effect does not mean that we are totally responsible for the behavior of others, or that we can control their actions. Each individual has their own free will and their own life journey. However, what we project into relationships creates an energy field, an emotional atmosphere, that influences the dynamics of interaction and attracts corresponding experiences to us. It is like a feedback loop: our projection influences the other person's behavior, which in turn reinforces our initial projection, creating a self-perpetuating relational pattern.

Principles for Co-creating Harmonious Relationships

To co-create more harmonious, loving, and enriching relationships, we can apply the following principles of conscious co-creation:

Clarity of Relational Intention: Just as we set clear intentions for the areas of our lives that we wish to manifest, we can also set clear intentions for our relationships. Ask yourself: "What kind of relationships do I want to co-create in my life? What qualities do I value in a relationship? How do I want to feel and be treated in my relationships? What kind of energy do I want to radiate to my relationships?". Set clear and specific intentions for your relationships, focusing on the qualities of harmony, love, connection, understanding, respect, support, mutual growth, and shared joy.

Projecting Unconditional Love and Acceptance: The foundation of harmonious relationships is unconditional love and acceptance. Seek to project unconditional love and acceptance to the people in your life, recognizing their inherent perfection, their unique qualities, and their unlimited potential, even beyond their imperfections and human limitations. Send thoughts of love, compassion, and kindness to the people you relate to, visualizing them happy, healthy, and fulfilled. Your projection of unconditional love creates an energy field of acceptance and openness, which invites others to respond in the same way.

Cultivating Empathy and Understanding: Harmony in relationships flourishes with empathy and mutual understanding. Try to put yourself in the other person's shoes, try to understand their perspective, their feelings, their needs, and their motives, even when you disagree with their point of view or do not understand their actions. Practice active listening, listening attentively and presently to what the other person has to say, without judgment or interruption. Empathy and understanding create bridges of connection and compassion, dissolving barriers and conflicts.

Communicating with Clarity, Honesty, and Kindness: Communication is the backbone of any healthy and harmonious relationship. Seek to communicate with clarity, honesty, and kindness in all your interactions. Express your thoughts, feelings, and needs assertively, but respectfully, without aggression or passivity. Avoid judgments, criticisms, and accusations, and try to focus on expressing your feelings ("I feel...") and your needs ("I need...") instead of blaming or attacking the other person. Clear, honest, and kind communication builds trust, understanding, and intimacy in relationships.

Focusing on Strengths and Positive Qualities: Instead of focusing on the flaws, failures, or negative behaviors of the people you relate to, try to direct your focus to their strengths, their positive qualities, and their potential. Recognize and appreciate the virtues, talents, and positive contributions of the people in your life, and express your recognition and gratitude for them. Your focus on the positive aspects strengthens the positive qualities in others, and creates a virtuous cycle of appreciation and mutual appreciation.

Forgiving and Releasing Resentments: In all relationships, there are inevitably moments of misunderstanding, conflict, and pain. The key to maintaining harmony in the long run is the ability to forgive and release resentments. Resentment and grudges poison relationships, erode connection, and block the flow of love. Practice conscious forgiveness, freeing yourself from the need to be right, to take revenge, or to punish the other person. Forgive not only the other person, but also yourself, for your own flaws and imperfections. Forgiveness releases the past, opens space for the present, and builds a lighter and more harmonious relational future.

Cultivating Gratitude in Relationships: Gratitude is a magical ingredient to strengthen and nurture relationships. Practice conscious gratitude in your relationships, expressing your appreciation and recognition for the people in your life, for their qualities, for their actions, for their contributions, and for their presence on your journey. Say "thank you" sincerely, send messages of appreciation, write letters of gratitude, offer small gestures of recognition. Gratitude in relationships nurtures love, strengthens connection, and attracts more reasons to be grateful in the relational dynamic.

Practices for Co-creating Harmonious Relationships

To integrate the principles of conscious co-creation into your relationships, try the following practices:

Meditation of Unconditional Love and Compassion: Set aside daily time for meditation on unconditional love and compassion. Sit in silence, breathe deeply, and direct thoughts of love, kindness, and compassion to the people in your life, starting with yourself, then your family, friends, colleagues, acquaintances, strangers, and even to the people with whom you have conflicts or difficulties. Visualize them happy, healthy, fulfilled, and at peace. Feel the emotion of unconditional love filling your heart and radiating out into the world, creating an energy field of harmony and relational well-being.

Affirmations for Harmonious Relationships: Use affirmations to strengthen the projection of harmonious relationships. Examples of affirmations: "I co-create harmonious, loving, and meaningful relationships", "I project unconditional love and acceptance to all my relationships", "I communicate with clarity, honesty, and kindness in all my interactions", "I cultivate empathy and understanding in my relationships", "I forgive and release resentments, opening space for love and harmony", "I am grateful for all the positive and enriching relationships in my life". Repeat these affirmations daily, with conviction and positive emotion, to program your subconscious mind with the intention of co-creating harmonious relationships.

Visualization of Harmonious Interactions: Use creative visualization to imagine harmonious interactions with the people in your life, especially those with whom you have challenges or difficulties. Visualize yourself dialoguing with clarity, respect, and understanding, resolving conflicts peacefully and constructively, sharing moments of joy, connection, and intimacy. Feel the positive emotions of harmony, peace, and joy filling your visualized interaction. Visualization of harmonious interactions programs your subconscious mind with positive expectations and prepares you to respond more harmoniously in real interactions.

Active Empathy Practice: Challenge yourself to practice active empathy in all your daily interactions. Before responding or reacting in a conversation, pause consciously and try to put yourself in the other person's shoes. Ask yourself: "What would it be like to be in this person's perspective? What might they be feeling? What might their needs and concerns be?". Listen attentively and presently, seeking to understand beyond words, the underlying emotion and intention. Respond with compassion, kindness, and understanding, seeking to build bridges of connection and empathy.

Daily Relational Gratitude Act: Choose a conscious relational gratitude act to practice every day. It can be verbally expressing your gratitude to someone, sending a message of appreciation, offering a gesture of affection, giving a sincere compliment, dedicating quality time to a loved one, etc. Small acts of relational gratitude nurture relationships, strengthen connection, and radiate positive energy to your interactions.

Co-creating harmonious relationships is an art that develops with awareness, intention, and practice. By applying the principles of conscious co-creation in your relationships, by projecting unconditional love, acceptance, understanding, clear communication, focus on the positive aspects, forgiveness, and gratitude, you can transform the dynamics of your interactions and create deeper, more meaningful relationships. and harmonious. Start co-creating more loving and enriching relationships today, and prepare to experience the joy, connection, and harmony that flourish when we project the best of ourselves in our interactions with others!

Chapter 20
Projecting Fulfillment and Contribution

Full fulfillment arises when we align our life purpose with our daily actions, transforming talents and passions into meaningful contributions to the world. More than a fixed destination, purpose is a journey of discovery and authentic expression, shaped by clear intention and inspired action. By opening ourselves to this conscious co-creation, we allow opportunities, connections, and experiences to flow naturally, manifesting a professional and personal trajectory full of meaning, abundance, and positive impact.

Life purpose and career are not just separate areas of our existence, but rather interconnected and interdependent dimensions that profoundly influence our well-being, our happiness, and our sense of fulfillment. Living a clear and meaningful life purpose, and dedicating our energy and talents to a career aligned with that purpose, is fundamental to a full, vibrant life with deep meaning. When our career becomes an expression of our life purpose, work ceases to be just an obligation or a means of subsistence, and transforms into a source of passion, joy, creativity, contribution, and personal fulfillment.

The good news is that life purpose and career can also be consciously co-created. Just as we shape other areas of our reality through our mental projection, we can also actively influence the discovery of our life purpose and the manifestation of a career aligned with our essence. By applying the principles of conscious co-creation to the domain of purpose and career, we can unleash our maximum potential, live a life with deep meaning, and leave a positive mark on the world.

Unveiling Life Purpose: A Journey of Inner Discovery

Life purpose is not something that is "found" like a lost object, or "discovered" like a predefined magic formula. Life purpose is something that unfolds gradually, that is revealed along the journey, that is consciously co-created in alignment with our essence, with our deepest values, with our unique talents, and with the guidance of our soul. The discovery of life purpose is a journey of self-knowledge, introspection, inner listening, and response to the calls of our soul.

Life purpose is not necessarily a great grandiose mission or a specific predetermined vocation. Life purpose can manifest itself in many ways: through a meaningful career, passionate volunteer work, creative projects that inspire us, deep relationships that nurture our soul, a way of life that resonates with our values, or a unique combination of all these dimensions. The important thing is not to "find" a specific pre-defined purpose, but to live a life with meaning, with passion, with joy, and with contribution, expressing our unique essence and our maximum potential in the world.

Principles for Co-creating Life Purpose and Aligned Career

To co-create a clear and meaningful life purpose and a career aligned with our essence, we can apply the following principles of conscious co-creation:

Clear Intention for Purpose and Career: Start by setting clear and specific intentions for your life purpose and your career. Ask yourself: "What is the greater purpose I wish to live in this life? What kind of impact do I wish to make in the world? What kind of work brings me joy, fulfillment, and meaning? What kind of career allows me to express my talents and passions? What kind of abundance do I want to attract through my career?". Set clear and specific intentions, focusing on what truly resonates with your soul, your values, and your deepest desires.

Connecting with Essence and Unique Talents: Dedicate time to self-connection and introspection to unveil your unique essence, your natural talents, your innate passions, and your deepest values. Ask yourself: "Who am I truly, beyond social roles and external expectations? What are my talents and natural abilities? What makes me feel alive, enthusiastic, and passionate? What are my most important values and what really matters to me in life?". Explore your passions, your interests, your past experiences, your dreams, and your deepest aspirations. The deeper your self-knowledge, the clearer your life purpose will become and the more aligned your career will be.

Visualize Life and Career Aligned with Purpose: Use creative visualization to imagine your life and career aligned with your life purpose. Visualize yourself living your purpose with passion, joy, and fulfillment, using your unique talents to contribute to the world in meaningful ways, experiencing financial abundance and professional recognition, feeling fulfilled and happy with your work. Engage all your senses and emotions in the visualization, making the image of your life and career aligned with purpose as vivid and real as possible.

Affirmations for Purpose and Aligned Career: Use affirmations to program your subconscious mind with empowering beliefs about your life purpose and career. Examples of affirmations: "I co-create a clear and meaningful life purpose", "I live my life purpose with passion, joy, and fulfillment", "I manifest a career aligned with my talents and passions", "I use my unique talents to contribute to the world in a meaningful way", "I attract financial abundance and professional recognition through my purpose-aligned career", "I am grateful to live a life full of purpose, passion, and professional fulfillment". Repeat these affirmations daily, with conviction and positive emotion, to strengthen your mental projection.

Inspired Action Toward Purpose and Career: Be aware of the impulses of inspired action that guide you toward your life purpose and aligned career. Follow your intuition, explore new areas of interest, try different activities, talk to people who inspire you, seek opportunities that resonate with your passion. Move forward with confidence and enthusiasm towards the paths that open before you, even if the final direction is not entirely clear at first. Inspired action is the compass that guides you to your life purpose.

Surrender to Divine Flow and the Wisdom of the Universe: Trust that the universe is conspiring in your favor to guide you in discovering your life purpose and manifesting your aligned career. Surrender your doubts, your fears, and your uncertainties to the universe, trusting that divine wisdom will reveal the right path at the perfect time and in the most appropriate way. Be open to surprises, synchronicities, and unexpected twists and turns that may arise along the journey. Surrendering to the divine flow allows the universe to guide you beyond your limited plans, to a higher and more meaningful destiny.

Cultivating Patience and Persistence on the Journey: Discovering life purpose and manifesting an aligned career are gradual and continuous processes that require time, patience, persistence, and self-compassion. Don't expect to find your purpose "overnight", or manifest the perfect career instantly. Allow yourself to explore, experiment, learn from mistakes, adjust course, and celebrate each step of the journey. Stay persistent in your practice of conscious co-creation, trust the process, and celebrate small progress along the way.

Practices for Co-creating Life Purpose and Aligned Career

To integrate the principles of conscious co-creation in the domain of life purpose and career, try the following practices:

Life Purpose Discovery Meditation: Set aside regular time for meditation on discovering life purpose.

Sit in silence, take a deep breath, and connect with your deepest essence. Ask your heart: "What is my life purpose? What did I come here to do? How can I contribute to the world in a meaningful way?". Be receptive to the answers that arise in your mind, your heart, and your intuition, and write down the ideas, insights, and feelings you receive.

Passion and Talents Exercise: Perform an exercise in exploring your passions and talents. Make a list of all the activities, themes, interests, hobbies that make you feel enthusiastic, joyful, and passionate. Identify your natural talents, your innate abilities, the areas where you feel most competent and fulfilled. Look for patterns and connections between your passions and talents, and reflect on how you might combine them to create a life purpose and career aligned with your essence.

Purpose Journey Journal: Keep a journal of your life purpose journey. Write down your reflections, your insights, your inspirations, your progress, your challenges, and your learnings throughout the journey of discovering purpose and co-creating career. This journal will help you track your progress, clarify your thoughts, strengthen your intention, and celebrate milestones on your journey.

Inspiring Conversations and Mentoring: Seek inspiring conversations with people who are already living their life purpose and have manifested careers aligned with their essence. Ask for advice, share your doubts and challenges, learn from their experiences and insights. Consider seeking a mentor who can guide and support you on the journey of discovering purpose and co-creating career. The wisdom and support of others can be invaluable to your growth and clarity of direction.

Weekly Act of Courage and Exploration: Challenge yourself to take an act of courage and exploration per week toward your life purpose and aligned career. It could be trying a new activity, attending an inspiring event, contacting someone you admire, starting a creative project, volunteering for a cause you're passionate about, taking an online course, reading an inspiring book, etc. . Small acts of courage and exploration open doors, reveal new possibilities, and propel your purpose journey.

Co-creating life purpose and aligned career is one of the greatest adventures of human existence, a journey of self-discovery, personal growth, and contribution to the world. By applying the principles of conscious co-creation to this fundamental domain, by projecting clear intentions, connecting with your essence, visualizing the desired reality, using empowering affirmations, following inspired action, surrendering to divine flow, and cultivating patience and persistence, you can discover your unique life purpose, manifest a career aligned with your essence, and live a life full of meaning, passion, and fulfillment. Start co-creating your life purpose and aligned career today, and prepare to blossom to your full potential, radiating your unique light to the world!

Chapter 21
Living a Projected Reality

The reality we experience is a direct reflection of our inner projections, a construct shaped by our thoughts, beliefs, and emotions. Every element of our existence, from challenges to achievements, is generated by how we interact energetically with the universe. True mastery of conscious co-creation goes beyond the simple manifestation of specific desires; it is about living in alignment with a continuous flow of clear intentions and inspired actions. By recognizing and assuming the role of projectors of our own reality, we take an essential step in transforming co-creation from a theoretical concept into a daily practice integrated into every moment of our lives.

Now, let's integrate all these tools and principles into our daily lives, transforming conscious co-creation from a sporadic or conceptual practice into a way of being and living, into a mastery of conscious projection that manifests in every moment and in all areas of our experience. The ultimate goal of conscious co-creation is not just to manifest isolated desires or achieve specific goals, but to live a masterfully projected life, a life full of meaning, joy, abundance, love, purpose, and fulfillment, in alignment with our deepest essence and the flow of life.

Conscious Co-creation as a Lifestyle

Integrating conscious co-creation into everyday life means incorporating its principles and practices into all dimensions of our experience, transforming the way we think, feel, act, and interact with the world. It is not about "adding" another technique or routine to our schedule, but about reconfiguring our consciousness, reprogramming our mental and emotional habits, redefining our paradigm of reality, and embracing a new way of being that manifests in all areas of our lives.

Conscious co-creation as a lifestyle implies:

Living in the Awareness of the Inner Projector: Always keep in mind the awareness of your power as an Inner Projector, constantly reminding yourself that you are the creator of your reality, that your thoughts, beliefs, intentions, and emotions actively shape your experience. Wake up each morning with the conscious intention of projecting a wonderful day, full of joy, abundance, and synchronicity, and remind yourself throughout the day of your power to influence your reality in every moment.

Cultivating Mindfulness and Presence: Living in the present moment with mindfulness and conscious presence is fundamental for daily co-creation. Practice mindfulness in all your daily activities, paying full attention to your sensations, your thoughts, your emotions, the environment around you, the taste of food, the touch of water, the sound of voices, etc. Conscious presence allows you to observe your thoughts and emotions without judgment, identify limiting patterns, direct your attention to the positive, and respond more consciously and intentionally to the challenges and opportunities that arise in your daily life.

Practicing Conscious Management of Thoughts and Beliefs: Maintain constant vigilance over your thoughts and beliefs, applying the techniques of identifying, dismantling, and replacing limiting beliefs that we explored in Chapter 10. Automatically transform negative thoughts into positive thoughts, limiting beliefs into empowering beliefs, fear into love, doubt into trust. Make conscious management of thoughts and beliefs a mental habit, a continuous practice of self-observation and self-transformation.

Incorporating Visualization and Affirmations into your Daily Routine: Integrate creative visualization and positive affirmations into your daily routine, making them habitual and automatic practices. Visualize the desired reality while brushing your teeth, showering, walking, waiting in traffic, or before falling asleep. Repeat your positive affirmations mentally or aloud while getting dressed, making coffee, exercising, or whenever you have a free moment. The more integrated and automatic the practices of visualization and affirmations become, the more powerful and constant your mental projection will be.

Living in Continuous Gratitude: Cultivate gratitude as a permanent mental attitude, a way of seeing the world and experiencing life. Begin and end each day with expressions of gratitude, recognizing and appreciating the blessings in your life, big and small.

Look for reasons to be grateful in all situations, even challenging or negative ones. Transform gratitude into a filter of perception, an emotional habit, a continuous dance of recognition and appreciation for the abundance of life.

Radiating Positive Emotions to the World: Make a conscious effort to cultivate and radiate positive emotions to the world in all your interactions. Consciously choose joy, love, enthusiasm, compassion, hope, trust, and peace as the predominant emotional states in your daily life. Practice kindness, generosity, and empathy in all your relationships, radiating positive energy to the people, places, and situations that surround you. Become a "focus of light" that radiates positivity to the world, attracting to you experiences and people that resonate with that same vibrant energy.

Dancing with Surrender and the Flow of Life: Live in the dance of surrender, trusting the flow of the universe, releasing excessive control and attachment to outcomes, accepting the present moment, listening to intuition, and following inner guidance. Flow with the natural rhythm of life, with its ups and downs, with its cycles of creation and destruction, with its unexpected twists and turns. Trust that the universe is conspiring in your favor, even when the path becomes winding or uncertain. Live with lightness, flexibility, and adaptability, dancing with life instead of fighting against it.

Acting Inspired and Aligned with Purpose: Take inspired decisions and actions, guided by intuition, enthusiasm, joy, and alignment with your life purpose.

Respond spontaneously to creative impulses, opportunities that arise, and synchronicities that manifest. Live with courage, authenticity, and passion, expressing your unique talents and contributing to the world in a meaningful way. Make inspired action a way of life, a continuous dance of creation and manifestation in the world.

Co-creating Harmonious Relationships in All Areas: Apply the principles of conscious co-creation to all your relationships, cultivating the projection of unconditional love, acceptance, empathy, understanding, clear communication, focus on the positive aspects, forgiveness, and gratitude in all your interactions. Radiate harmony and connection to your family, friends, colleagues, partners, acquaintances, and even strangers. Make harmonious relationships a priority in your life, recognizing that the quality of your interactions profoundly influences your well-being and happiness.

Manifesting Life Purpose and Aligned Career as an Expression of Essence: Live your life purpose and your aligned career as a natural expression of your essence, your unique talents, your innate passions, and your deepest values. Use your work as a vehicle for contributing to the world, as a way to leave your positive mark, as a source of joy, fulfillment, and abundance. Integrate your life purpose and your aligned career into all dimensions of your existence, living a coherent, authentic, and meaningful life.

Practical Tips for Continuous Integration

To facilitate the continuous integration of conscious co-creation into your daily life, try the following practical tips:

Start Small and Be Gradual: Don't try to transform your life overnight. Start with small changes, focusing on integrating one or two principles or practices of conscious co-creation into your daily routine. As you feel more comfortable and confident, gradually add new elements and expand your practice to other areas of your life. Consistency and gradual progression are more effective than radical and ephemeral attempts at change.

Set Visual and Auditory Reminders: Create visual and auditory reminders to help you stay aware of co-creation throughout the day. Use post-it notes with positive affirmations on your mirror, refrigerator, or computer. Set alarms on your cell phone with inspirational messages or reminders to practice gratitude or visualization. Use wallpapers on your computer or cell phone with images that represent the reality you want to co-create. Visual and auditory reminders help keep your attention focused on conscious co-creation throughout the day.

Create Daily and Weekly Rituals: Incorporate daily and weekly rituals into your routine to reinforce the practice of conscious co-creation. Set aside specific times of the day for meditation, visualization, affirmations, writing in the gratitude journal, or other practices that resonate with you. Set times of the week to reflect on your progress, plan your intentions, celebrate your achievements, and adjust your approach.

Daily and weekly rituals create structure, consistency, and discipline in your conscious co-creation practice.

Find an Accountability Partner or Support Group: Find an accountability partner or join a conscious co-creation support group to share experiences, challenges, achievements, and learning, to receive and offer encouragement and motivation, and to stay accountable for your practice. Sharing with others who are on a similar path can strengthen your determination, expand your perspective, and enrich your journey.

Be Patient, Kind, and Persistent with Yourself: Remember that integrating conscious co-creation into everyday life is a continuous and gradual process, not a goal to be achieved instantly or perfectly. Be patient, kind, and compassionate with yourself along the way. Don't criticize yourself for your "slips" or your difficulties. Celebrate small progress, learn from challenges, and persist in your practice with love, faith, and determination. Mastery of conscious co-creation is a life journey, not a final destination.

Integrating conscious co-creation into everyday life is embracing a new way of being and living, a more conscious, more intentional, more empowered, more abundant, and more joyful way. It is transforming your reality from the inside out, masterfully projecting the life of your dreams, and living each moment with presence, gratitude, joy, purpose, and love. Start integrating conscious co-creation into your daily life today, and prepare to witness an extraordinary transformation of your experience as you become a master of conscious projection and dance in perfect harmony with the universe, co-creating a reality full of beauty, abundance, and fulfillment!

Chapter 22
Co-creating Health

Health is a natural expression of the balance between body, mind, emotions, and spirit, reflecting the inner harmony that we project into our reality. More than just the absence of disease, true health manifests as vitality, energy, and well-being in all areas of life. Every thought, belief, and emotion directly influences our physical state, activating mechanisms of regeneration or imbalance. By recognizing our power of co-creation, we can align ourselves with patterns that strengthen our health, promoting a state of fullness and natural self-regulation, where vitality flows as a reflection of our inner alignment.

The good news is that radiant health and complete well-being can be consciously co-created. Just as we shape other areas of our reality through our mental projection, we can also actively influence our health and well-being through our thoughts, beliefs, intentions, emotions, and actions aligned with vitality and harmony. By understanding the principles of conscious co-creation applied to health and well-being, we can become more skilled and responsible co-creators of our own journey of healing, vitality, and wholeness.

Health as a Natural State of Being: A Return to Harmony

It is essential to understand that radiant health is our natural state of being. Our body is a perfect machine of self-healing and self-regulation, intrinsically programmed for vitality and balance. Disease and imbalance are not "normal" or "inevitable" states, but rather signs of misalignment with our natural state of harmony, often caused by patterns of thought, beliefs, emotions, and lifestyles that do not support our vitality.

Conscious co-creation of radiant health and complete well-being is, therefore, a process of returning to harmony, of realigning with our natural state of vitality, of removing the blocks and resistances that distance us from our innate well-being. It is a process of awakening to the intrinsic wisdom of our body, of honoring its innate intelligence, and of consciously collaborating with its mechanisms of self-healing and self-regulation.

Principles for Co-creating Radiant Health and Complete Well-being

To co-create radiant health and complete well-being in all dimensions of your being, we can apply the following principles of conscious co-creation:

Clear Intention for Health and Well-being: Start by setting clear and specific intentions for your health and well-being. Ask yourself: "What does radiant health and complete well-being look like to me? How do I want to feel physically, mentally, emotionally, and spiritually? What level of vitality and energy do I want to experience? What kind of health do I want to manifest in my body? What kind of well-being do I want to radiate into my life?" Define clear and specific intentions, focusing on a vibrant state of health and well-being in all dimensions of your being.

Projecting Images of Perfect Health and Vitality: Use creative visualization to project vivid and detailed images of yourself enjoying perfect health and radiant vitality. Visualize your body strong, healthy, energized, flexible, resilient, and vibrant. Imagine your organs functioning in perfect harmony, your cells glowing with vital energy, your immune system robust and efficient, your mind clear, focused, and calm, your emotions balanced and harmonious, your spirit full of peace, joy, and connection. Involve all your senses in the visualization, seeing, hearing, feeling, smelling, and tasting the experience of radiant health and complete well-being.

Affirmations for Radiant Health and Complete Well-being: Use positive and empowering affirmations to program your subconscious mind with beliefs of health, vitality, and well-being. Examples of affirmations: "I co-create radiant health and complete well-being in all dimensions of my being," "I have perfect health and vibrant vitality," "My body is strong, healthy, energized, and resilient," "My cells regenerate and revitalize constantly," "My immune system is strong and efficient," "My mind is clear, focused, and calm," "My emotions are balanced and harmonious," "My spirit is full of peace, joy, and connection," "I am grateful for my perfect health and complete well-being." Repeat these affirmations daily, with conviction and positive emotion, to strengthen your mental projection.

Cultivating Positive Emotions of Health and Well-being: Seek to cultivate and maintain positive emotions associated with health and well-being, such as joy, gratitude, enthusiasm, love, trust, inner peace, vitality, and energy. Feel these emotions filling your body and vibrating in every cell of your being. Positive emotions raise your vibrational frequency, attuning you to the energy of health and well-being, and strengthening your ability to manifest these qualities in your reality.

Nourishing the Body with Conscious Nutrition and Vitality: Conscious and vitalizing nutrition is a fundamental pillar of co-creating radiant health. Choose nutritious, whole, organic, and vibrant foods, rich in vitamins, minerals, antioxidants, and vital energy. Prioritize fruits, vegetables, legumes, whole grains, seeds, nuts, and lean proteins. Reduce or eliminate processed, refined, sugary, fatty, and toxic foods that drain your energy and harm your health. Eat with mindfulness, savoring each meal, giving thanks for the food, and nourishing your body with love and respect.

Moving the Body with Joy and Awareness: Conscious and enjoyable movement is essential for radiant health and complete well-being. Choose physical activities that bring you joy, pleasure, and vitality, that resonate with your essence, and that adapt to your needs and abilities. Walk in nature, dance, swim, practice yoga, do tai chi, ride a bike, run, do strength training, or any other activity that makes you feel alive, energized, and connected to your body. Move with body awareness, paying attention to the sensations, limits, and signals of your body, honoring its rhythm and needs.

Resting and Regenerating the Body and Mind: Adequate rest and regeneration are fundamental for radiant health and complete well-being. Allow your body and mind to rest and regenerate during sleep, leisure, relaxation, and meditation. Prioritize restful sleep, with 7-9 hours of deep and restful sleep per night. Set aside daily time for conscious relaxation, pleasurable leisure, meditation, and silent contemplation, allowing your nervous system to calm down, your cells to revitalize, and your mind to renew itself.

Connecting with Nature and Vital Energy: Connection with nature and vital energy is essential for radiant health and complete well-being. Spend time regularly in contact with nature, in natural and invigorating environments such as parks, gardens, forests, beaches, mountains, lakes, rivers, etc. Absorb the vital energy of the sun, fresh air, fresh water, fertile earth, plants, and animals. Nature nourishes the body, calms the mind, elevates the spirit, and revitalizes vital energy.

Cultivating Healthy Relationships and Social Support: Healthy relationships and social support are fundamental for emotional and mental well-being, which in turn influence physical health. Cultivate positive, nurturing, loving, and supportive relationships with family, friends, partners, and communities that inspire, value, and uplift you. Invest time and energy in meaningful social connections, share moments of joy, support, and intimacy with the people you love. Healthy relationships and social support are pillars of complete well-being.

Living with Purpose, Meaning, and Contribution: Living a life with purpose, meaning, and contribution is essential for spiritual health and existential well-being, which also influence physical, mental, and emotional health. Discover your unique life purpose, what makes you feel alive, passionate, and fulfilled, what motivates you to get out of bed every day with enthusiasm. Dedicate time and energy to activities that resonate with your purpose, that express your talents and passions, and that contribute to the greater good of the world. Living with purpose, meaning, and contribution nourishes the soul, strengthens the spirit, and radiates well-being into all areas of life.

Practices for Co-creating Radiant Health and Complete Well-being

To integrate the principles of conscious co-creation into your journey of radiant health and complete well-being, try the following practices:

Meditation of Healing and Vitality: Set aside daily time for meditation of healing and vitality. Sit in silence, breathe deeply, and visualize golden light and vital energy filling your body, revitalizing every cell, harmonizing every organ, strengthening your immune system, and restoring your natural balance and well-being. Repeat affirmations of health and vitality during meditation, and feel the emotion of healing and well-being filling your being.

Health and Wellness Journal: Keep a health and wellness journal where you daily record your progress, insights, learning, and intentions on the journey of co-creating radiant health. Write down your practices of conscious nutrition, movement, rest, connection with nature, meditation, affirmations, visualizations, and cultivation of positive emotions. Celebrate small victories, acknowledge your efforts, and adjust your approach as needed.

Creating a Health and Wellness Action Plan: Create a concrete and realistic action plan to integrate the principles of conscious co-creation into your health and wellness journey. Set specific, measurable, achievable, relevant, and time-bound (SMART) goals for each area of your life (nutrition, movement, rest, etc.). Establish practical and gradual steps to implement the desired changes, and track your progress over time.

Consultation with Conscious Health Professionals: Seek guidance and support from conscious and integrative health professionals who understand the importance of mind, body, emotions, and spirit in the journey of healing and well-being. Consult with doctors, nutritionists, therapists, wellness coaches, yoga teachers, meditation teachers, or other integrative practitioners who can complement your conscious co-creation practice and guide you in a personalized way on your journey of radiant health.

Health and Wellness Support Community: Join a health and wellness support community, online or in person, to share experiences, receive support, exchange ideas, get inspired, and motivate each other on the journey of co-creating radiant health. The support and sharing with others who are on a similar path can strengthen your determination and enrich your experience.

Co-creating radiant health and complete well-being is a holistic, continuous, and profoundly transformative process that involves the mind, body, emotions, and spirit. By applying the principles of conscious co-creation to your health journey, by projecting clear intentions, visualizing vitality, using empowering affirmations, cultivating positive emotions, nourishing the body, moving with joy, resting and regenerating, connecting with nature, cultivating healthy relationships, and living with purpose, you can awaken your innate potential for self-healing and self-regulation, manifest vibrant health and complete well-being in all dimensions of your being, and live a life full of vitality, energy, joy, and fulfillment. Start co-creating your radiant health and complete well-being today, and prepare to flourish in all your potential for vitality and wholeness!

Chapter 23
Co-creating Abundance

Abundance is a natural flow of the universe, an energy available to all who align with its frequency. True prosperity goes beyond the possession of material goods, reflecting a state of fullness in all areas of life - financial, emotional, relational, and spiritual. Money, as an expression of the energy of abundance, responds to the beliefs and emotions we project onto it. By transforming limiting patterns and cultivating a mindset of wealth, we can open the doors to a continuous flow of opportunities, resources, and experiences that sustain a prosperous and meaningful life.

Many people struggle with financial scarcity, living in worry, limitation, and stress in relation to money. The belief in scarcity is a limiting mental program that prevents us from recognizing and attracting the abundance that is naturally ours by divine right. The good news is that financial abundance and prosperity can be consciously co-created, just like any other area of our reality. By transforming our limiting beliefs about money, aligning our energy with the frequency of abundance, and applying the tools of conscious co-creation, we can open the flow of prosperity in all areas of our lives.

Abundance as the Natural State of the Universe: Unblocking the Divine Flow

It is crucial to understand that the universe is intrinsically abundant. Nature is lavish in resources, beauty, life, and energy. Scarcity is an illusion of the egoic mind, a distorted perception of reality, fueled by limiting beliefs and negative thought patterns. Abundance is the natural state of the universe, and it is available to all of us in unlimited quantities.

The conscious co-creation of financial abundance and prosperity is, therefore, a process of unblocking the divine flow, of removing the mental, emotional, and energetic barriers that prevent us from receiving the abundance that is naturally ours. It is a process of realigning with the frequency of prosperity, of opening to receptivity, and of allowing abundance to flow freely into our lives.

Principles for Co-creating Financial Abundance and Prosperity:

To co-create financial abundance and prosperity in all areas of your life, we can apply the following principles of conscious co-creation:

Clear Intention for Abundance and Prosperity: Begin by setting clear and specific intentions for your financial abundance and prosperity. Ask yourself: "What does financial abundance and prosperity look like to me? What level of financial wealth do I want to manifest in my life? What kind of opportunities and resources do I want to attract? How do I want to feel about money and prosperity? What kind of abundance do I want to experience in all areas of my life?" Set clear and specific intentions, focusing on a vibrant state of abundance and prosperity in all dimensions of your being.

Transform Limiting Beliefs About Money: Identify and transform your limiting beliefs about money, the negative beliefs that prevent you from attracting and receiving financial abundance. Beliefs such as "money is dirty", "money is the root of all evil", "I don't deserve to be rich", "you have to work hard to earn money", "abundance is for others, not for me", "there is not enough money for everyone", are mental blocks that sabotage your prosperity. Use the techniques for releasing limiting beliefs that we explored in Chapter 10 to dismantle these negative beliefs and replace them with empowering beliefs about money, such as "money is energy", "money is a tool for good", "I deserve to be rich and prosperous," "money flows easily and abundantly into my life", "abundance is my natural state", "there is unlimited abundance for everyone".

Visualize Financial Abundance and Prosperity: Use creative visualization to project vivid and detailed images of yourself enjoying financial abundance and prosperity in all areas of your life. Visualize yourself living with comfort, security, and financial freedom, having resources to fulfill your dreams and desires, contributing to causes that inspire you, enjoying enriching experiences, sharing your abundance with others. Imagine your bank account full, your wallet prosperous, your opportunities flowing easily, your investments prospering, your business flourishing. Engage all your senses in visualization, seeing, hearing, feeling, smelling, and tasting the experience of financial abundance and prosperity.

Affirmations for Financial Abundance and Prosperity: Use positive and empowering affirmations to program your subconscious mind with beliefs of abundance and financial prosperity. Examples of affirmations: "I co-create financial abundance and prosperity in all areas of my life", "I am a magnet for financial abundance and prosperity", "Money flows easily and abundantly into my life", "I deserve to be rich and prosperous", "I am open and receptive to receiving abundance from all sources", "I use money wisely and generously for the greater good", "I am grateful for the financial abundance and prosperity that constantly flows into my life". Repeat these affirmations daily, with conviction and positive emotion, to strengthen your mental projection.

Cultivate Positive Emotions of Abundance and Prosperity: Seek to cultivate and maintain positive emotions associated with abundance and prosperity, such as joy, gratitude, enthusiasm, confidence, optimism, security, contentment, and appreciation for wealth. Feel these emotions filling your body and vibrating in every cell of your being. Positive emotions raise your vibrational frequency, tuning you into the energy of abundance and prosperity, and strengthening your ability to attract these qualities into your reality.

Practice Gratitude for Present and Future Abundance: Gratitude is a powerful magnet for abundance. Practice conscious gratitude for the abundance that already exists in your life, however small it may seem. Give thanks for the air you breathe, the water you drink, the food you eat, the home that shelters you, the clothes you wear, the people who love you, the opportunities that present themselves, the blessings that surround you. Also express gratitude in advance for the future abundance you are co-creating, as if it were already a present reality. Feel gratitude filling your heart and radiating out into the universe, opening the flow of abundance into your life.

Give and Receive with Balance and Generosity: Abundance flows in a continuous cycle of giving and receiving. To attract more financial abundance and prosperity, it is important to give generously and receive with gratitude, maintaining a balance between these two polarities. Give with joy and generosity, without attachment to the outcome, without expecting reward, with the intention of contributing to the greater good. Receive with gratitude and openness, recognizing your worthiness and deservingness to receive abundance, without guilt or resistance. The balance between giving and receiving keeps the flow of abundance in constant motion in your life.

Live with a Mindset of Abundance and Opportunity: Transform your scarcity mindset into an abundance mindset. Instead of focusing on lack, limitation, and competition, focus on abundance, opportunities, and cooperation. Believe that there is unlimited abundance for everyone, that the universe is prosperous and generous, that there is always more than enough to satisfy everyone's needs and desires. See the world as a place full of unlimited opportunities to create, to prosper, to contribute, to fulfill your dreams. The abundance mindset opens your eyes to opportunities and attracts prosperity into your life.

Take Inspired Action Aligned with Prosperity: Be attentive to the impulses of inspired action that guide you towards financial prosperity and abundance. Follow your intuition, explore new business opportunities, invest in your talents and passions, look for creative ways to generate value and contribute to the world, connect with prosperous and inspiring people, invest in your personal and professional development. Move with confidence and enthusiasm towards the paths that open before you, trusting in your ability to create abundance and prosperity in all areas of your life.

Manage Money with Awareness and Wisdom: Financial abundance is not just about attracting more money, but also about managing money with awareness and wisdom. Develop healthy financial habits such as saving, investing, planning, budgeting, and managing your money responsibly and intelligently. Learn to use money as a tool for good, to fulfill your dreams, to support your passions, to contribute to causes that inspire you, and to create more abundance for yourself and others. Conscious and wise money management strengthens your financial prosperity in the long term.

Practices for Co-creating Financial Abundance and Prosperity:

To integrate the principles of conscious co-creation into your journey of financial abundance and prosperity, try the following practices:

Abundance and Prosperity Meditation: Set aside daily time for abundance and prosperity meditation. Sit in silence, breathe deeply, and visualize yourself immersed in an ocean of financial abundance and prosperity. Feel the energy of wealth, opulence, financial freedom, and security enveloping your being. Repeat affirmations of abundance and prosperity during meditation, and feel the emotion of wealth and prosperity filling your heart.

Abundance and Prosperity Journal: Keep an abundance and prosperity journal, where you record daily your experiences, insights, learning, and intentions on the journey of co-creating financial abundance. Write down the opportunities that arise, the synchronicities you witness, your financial progress, your gratitude practices for present and future abundance, and your inspired actions towards prosperity. Celebrate small victories, acknowledge your efforts, and adjust your approach as needed.

Creating a Prosperity Vision Map: Create a prosperity vision map, a visual board that represents your vision of financial abundance and prosperity in all areas of your life. Paste images, phrases, words, symbols, colors, and objects that represent the wealth, opulence, financial freedom, opportunities, resources, and prosperity you want to manifest. Place your vision map in a visible location and be inspired by it daily, visualizing yourself living the prosperous reality you are co-creating.

Consult with Conscious Financial Coaches and Prosperity Mentors: Seek guidance and support from conscious financial coaches and prosperity mentors who understand the principles of conscious co-creation and who can guide you in a personalized way on your journey of financial abundance. Consult professionals who can help you transform your limiting beliefs about money, develop healthy financial habits, identify business opportunities, invest intelligently, and align your energy with the frequency of prosperity.

Prosperity Mastermind Group: Join a prosperity mastermind group, a circle of people with an abundance mindset and similar financial goals, to share ideas, strategies, resources, support, and networking. The collective energy and shared wisdom of a mastermind group can amplify your ability to co-create financial abundance and prosperity, accelerating your progress and expanding your possibilities.

Co-creating financial abundance and prosperity is a transformative and empowering process, which frees you from scarcity, limitation, and worry, and opens you to a world of unlimited opportunities, abundant resources, and financial and material fulfillment. By applying the principles of conscious co-creation to your journey of prosperity, transforming your limiting beliefs, visualizing abundance, using empowering affirmations, cultivating positive emotions, practicing gratitude, giving and receiving with balance, living with a mindset of abundance, taking inspired action, and managing money wisely, you can unlock the divine flow of prosperity in all areas of your life, manifest the financial abundance you desire and deserve, and live a life full of wealth, freedom, joy, and contribution. Start co-creating your financial abundance and prosperity today, and prepare to witness the magic of manifesting wealth and unlimited opportunities in your reality!

Chapter 24
Learning to Project Peace

Peace is an inner state that is reflected in the world around us, manifesting in our relationships, choices, and the environment in which we live. Projecting peace means intentionally cultivating harmony in the mind, balance in emotions, and serenity in the heart, allowing this energy to expand into every aspect of life. When we align with this frequency, our home becomes a haven of tranquility, our relationships flow with more understanding, and our path unfolds with ease. True peace is not the absence of challenges, but the presence of a consciousness that chooses to respond with clarity, love, and trust.

A harmonious home and a sacred space are not defined by size, luxury, or decoration, but by the energy that vibrates in the environment. It is a place that welcomes us with peace, beauty, serenity, comfort and security, a space that nourishes our soul, inspires our spirit and invites us to relax, regenerate and reconnect with our essence. The good news is that the harmony of the home and the creation of a sacred space can be consciously co-created, just like any other area of our reality. By applying the principles of conscious co-creation to our home, we can transform it into a true oasis of peace and well-being, a refuge that sustains and uplifts us at all times.

The Home as an Extension of Our Consciousness: Reflecting Our Inner Harmony

It is important to understand that our home is an extension of our consciousness, a reflection of our inner state, a mirror of our energy and our mental and emotional projections. If our inner self is in disorder, conflict, stress or negativity, it is likely that our home will reflect that same energy through disorganization, confusion, lack of harmony and an unwelcoming environment. If, on the other hand, we cultivate inner peace, harmony, serenity and positivity, it is more likely that our home will become a space that radiates those same qualities, creating an environment that nourishes and uplifts us.

The conscious co-creation of a harmonious home and a sacred space is, therefore, a process of inner and outer alignment, of harmonizing our consciousness with our physical environment, of intentional projection of energies of peace, beauty and security to our personal refuge. It is a process of making our home a reflection of our best version, a sanctuary that supports our personal growth, our happiness and our full well-being.

Principles for Co-creating a Harmonious Home and a Sacred Space:

To co-create a harmonious home and a sacred space that nourishes your soul, we can apply the following principles of conscious co-creation:

Clear Intention for Harmony and Sacred Space: Begin by setting clear and specific intentions for the harmony of your home and the creation of a sacred space. Ask yourself: "What does a harmonious home and a sacred space look like to me? How do I want to feel in my home? What kind of energy do I want to vibrate in my personal space? What qualities do I want my home to reflect? What kind of refuge do I want to co-create for myself and my loved ones?" Set clear and specific intentions, focusing on a home that is a true sanctuary of peace, beauty and security for yourself and all who dwell there.

Project Images of Peace, Beauty and Security in the Home: Use creative visualization to project vivid and detailed images of your home transformed into a harmonious and sacred space. Visualize each room in your home radiating peace, serenity, calm, beauty, light, order, cleanliness, comfort and security. Imagine the colors, natural light, objects, plants, sounds, scents, the general atmosphere of your home vibrating in perfect harmony and balance. Engage all your senses in visualization, seeing, hearing, feeling, smelling and savoring the experience of being in your harmonious home and sacred space.

Affirmations for Harmony and Sacred Space in the Home: Use positive and empowering affirmations to program your subconscious mind with beliefs of harmony and sacredness for your home. Examples of affirmations: "I co-create a harmonious home and a sacred space that nourishes my soul", "My home is a haven of peace, beauty and security", "The energy of my home is light, fluid and harmonious", "Each room in my house radiates calm, serenity and comfort", "My home is a sacred space where I feel loved, safe and protected", "I am grateful for my harmonious home and sacred space". Repeat these affirmations daily, with conviction and positive emotion, to strengthen your mental projection.

Cultivate Positive Emotions of Peace, Harmony and Security in the Home: Seek to cultivate and maintain positive emotions associated with peace, harmony and security in your home, such as joy, gratitude, love, serenity, calm, contentment, comfort, relaxation and well-being. Feel these emotions filling your body and vibrating in every cell of your being as you think about your home, as you visualize your transformed space, as you practice your affirmations. Positive emotions raise your vibrational frequency, tuning your home into the energy of harmony and sacredness, and strengthening your ability to manifest these qualities in your physical environment.

Detoxify and Energetically Cleanse the Home: Energetic cleansing of the home is essential to create a sacred space. Detoxify your home from negative, unnecessary or stagnant energies through energy cleansing practices such as: opening windows and ventilating the house, allowing fresh air and sunlight to enter and renew the energy of the environment; burning natural incense or sacred herbs like white sage, palo santo or lavender to purify and raise the vibration of the space; using harmonious sounds like relaxing music, mantras or Tibetan bowls to balance the energy of the home; physically cleaning and organizing the house, removing unnecessary objects, repairing damaged items, and creating order and fluidity in the environment.

Perform energy cleansing of your home regularly, especially when you feel the environment is heavy, tense or disharmonious.

Organize and Harmonize the Physical Space of the Home: The organization and harmonization of the physical space are essential to create a harmonious home and a sacred space. Organize each room in your home to create order, fluidity and functionality in the environment. Remove clutter, excess objects and visual confusion, creating space for energy to flow freely. Harmonize the decor using soft, relaxing colors, natural lighting, natural materials, plants, inspiring art objects, and decorative elements that resonate with your essence and your vision of a harmonious home. Create a visually pleasing, aesthetically balanced and functionally efficient environment that invites relaxation, well-being and inspiration.

Create Sacred Corners and Spaces for Introspection: Within your home, create sacred corners and spaces dedicated to introspection, meditation, prayer, relaxation and spiritual reconnection. It can be a small altar with meaningful objects, a quiet corner with cushions and candles, a reading space with inspiring books, an indoor garden with plants and flowers, a yoga or meditation studio, or any other space that resonates with your need for silence, introspection and reconnection with your essence. Use these sacred corners regularly to nourish your soul, calm your mind, uplift your spirit and strengthen your connection to your inner wisdom.

Infuse the Home with Elements of Nature and Vital Energy: Bring elements of nature into your home to infuse the environment with vital energy, freshness, beauty and natural harmony. Plants, flowers, crystals, stones, wood, water, sunlight, fresh air, sounds of nature (such as the sound of running water, wind or birds) are natural elements that raise the vibration of the home, purify the air, revitalize the energy of the environment, and connect us with the beauty and abundance of nature. Use these natural elements in decorating and organizing your home, creating an environment that breathes life, freshness and natural harmony.

Create a Welcoming and Inviting Atmosphere for Yourself and Others: The harmonious home and sacred space should be welcoming and inviting, both for yourself and for the people you love and welcome into your space. Create an atmosphere that radiates human warmth, comfort, kindness, hospitality, love and joy. Use warm and inviting colors, soft and welcoming light, soft and comfortable textures, pleasant and comforting scents, and objects that evoke happy memories and positive feelings. Create an environment where everyone feels welcome, loved, safe and at peace.

Maintain the Conscious Intention of Harmony and Sacredness in the Home: It is essential to maintain the conscious intention of harmony and sacredness in your home on an ongoing basis. Remind yourself daily of your intention to co-create a harmonious home and a sacred space, reinforcing your visualizations, affirmations and practices of energy cleansing and space organization. Cultivate mindfulness in your home, paying attention to the energy of the environment, your feelings when you are at home, and the small details that can contribute to the harmony and well-being of your personal space. Continuous maintenance of conscious intention is key to sustaining the harmony and sacredness of your home in the long term.

Practices for Co-creating a Harmonious Home and a Sacred Space:

To integrate the principles of conscious co-creation into your journey of creating a harmonious home and a sacred space, try the following practices:

Home Harmonization Meditation: Set aside regular time for home harmonization meditation. Sit in silence, breathe deeply and visualize white and golden light filling your entire home, purifying each room, harmonizing each object, raising the vibration of the environment, and creating an energy field of peace, beauty and security throughout your home. your personal space. Repeat affirmations of harmony and sacredness of the home during meditation, and feel the emotion of peace and well-being filling your heart and your home.

Conscious Home Harmonization Walk: Take a conscious home harmonization walk. Walk through each room of your house with mindfulness, observing the energy of the space, identifying areas that need cleaning, organization or harmonization, and sending intentions of peace, beauty and security to every corner of your home. Touch objects with love and gratitude, reorganize spaces with conscious intention, and visualize the energy of your home becoming lighter, more fluid and harmonious.

Weekly Home Cleaning and Harmonization Ritual: Create a weekly home cleaning and harmonization ritual. Set aside a time of the week to do a deep physical and energetic cleaning of your personal space, applying the practices of ventilation, incense, sounds, organization, decoration, and creating sacred corners that resonate with you. Transform cleaning and organizing your home into a conscious and intentional act of creating a sacred space, infusing each action with love, gratitude and the intention of harmonizing your environment

Vision Map of the Harmonious Home and Sacred Space: Create a vision map of the harmonious home and sacred space, a visual board that represents your vision of the ideal home, the perfect refuge, the personal sanctuary that you want to co-create. Paste images, phrases, words, symbols, colors and objects that represent the peace, beauty, security, comfort, harmony, light, nature and sacredness that you want to manifest in your home. Place your vision map in a visible location and be inspired by it daily, visualizing yourself living in the harmonious home and sacred space that you are co-creating.

Sharing the Intention to Co-create the Harmonious Home with Co-inhabitants: If you share your home with other people, share your intention to co-create a harmonious home and a sacred space with your co-inhabitants. Talk about your vision of an ideal home, listen to their perspectives, and try to find common ground and mutual agreement on creating a harmonious and welcoming environment for everyone. Invite your housemates to participate in the practices of energy cleansing, organization and decoration of the home, transforming the co-creation of the sacred space into a collaborative and enriching project for all.

Co-creating a harmonious home and a sacred space is an act of self-love, self-care and conscious creation of a personal refuge that sustains your life journey. By applying the principles of conscious co-creation to your home, projecting clear intentions, visualizing harmony, using empowering affirmations, cultivating positive emotions, cleaning and organizing the space, bringing nature indoors, and maintaining the conscious intention of sacredness, you can transform your home into a true sanctuary of peace, beauty and security, a space that nourishes your soul, uplifts your spirit and radiates well-being to all areas of your life. Start co-creating your harmonious home and sacred space today, and prepare to experience the joy, comfort and serenity of having a personal refuge that supports and uplifts you at all times!

Chapter 25
Co-creating Travels

Traveling is about expanding horizons, transforming perceptions, and allowing yourself to live experiences that nourish the soul. Each journey is more than just a change of location; it's an opportunity to connect with new cultures, landscapes, and above all, with yourself. When we align our intentions with the energy of discovery, our travels become filled with synchronicities, meaningful encounters, and unforgettable moments. Co-creating a trip isn't just about planning itineraries, but about opening yourself to the magic of the unknown, allowing each destination to reveal new possibilities for growth, inspiration, and enchantment.

Often, we plan trips based on logistics, budget, or external expectations, forgetting that travel can be much more than just tourist trips. The good news is that magical journeys and memorable experiences can be consciously co-created, just like any other area of our reality. By applying the principles of conscious co-creation to our travels, we can transform them into transformative adventures, journeys full of synchronicities, magical moments, inspiring encounters, and experiences that nourish our soul and expand our consciousness.

Traveling as a Soul Journey: Expanding Consciousness Through Adventure

It is important to understand that travel is, at its core, a journey of the soul, a search for expansion, growth, knowledge, beauty, connection, adventure, and meaning. Travel has the power to free us from routine, to challenge us to leave our comfort zone, to open us to new perspectives, to connect us with the diversity of the world, and to reconnect us with our own essence through the exploration of the unknown.

Conscious co-creation of magical journeys and memorable experiences is, therefore, a process of conscious intention, openness to the magic of synchronicity, trust in the flow of life, and permission for the journey to become a transformative journey that resonates with our soul and leaves us with precious memories for life.

Principles for Co-creating Magical Journeys and Memorable Experiences

To co-create magical journeys and memorable experiences that nourish your soul, you can apply the following principles of conscious co-creation:

Clear Intention for a Magical and Memorable Trip: Start by setting clear and specific intentions for your magical and memorable trip. Ask yourself: "What kind of trip do I want to co-create? What kind of experiences do I want to have? What kind of places do I want to explore? What kind of people do I want to meet? What kind of transformation do I want to achieve through this trip? What kind of memories do I want to create?" Set clear and specific intentions, focusing on the qualities of magic, adventure, beauty, discovery, transformation, connection, joy, and unforgettable memories that you want to experience on your trip.

Visualize the Magical Trip and Memorable Experiences: Use creative visualization to project vivid and detailed images of your magical trip and memorable experiences. Visualize yourself enjoying magical moments, stunning scenery, inspiring encounters, exciting adventures, enriching cultural experiences, moments of relaxation and rejuvenation, surprising synchronicities, and unforgettable memories. Imagine yourself feeling joy, enthusiasm, wonder, gratitude, inner peace, and deep connection with the world and yourself during your trip. Engage all your senses in visualization, seeing, hearing, feeling, smelling, and tasting the experience of your magical and memorable trip.

Affirmations for Magical Journeys and Memorable Experiences: Use positive and empowering affirmations to program your subconscious mind with beliefs about magic, adventure, and memorable experiences in your travels. Examples of affirmations: "I co-create magical journeys and memorable experiences that nourish my soul," "My travels are filled with joy, adventure, and beauty," "I attract synchronicities and magical moments on all my travels," "I connect with inspiring people and enriching cultures on my travels," "I create unforgettable and transformative memories on all my travels," "I am grateful for the magical journeys and memorable experiences that enrich my life." Repeat these affirmations daily, with conviction and positive emotion, to strengthen your mental projection.

Cultivate Positive Emotions of Adventure, Enthusiasm, and Gratitude for the Trip: Seek to cultivate and maintain positive emotions associated with adventure, enthusiasm, and gratitude for your trip, even before it begins. Feel the excitement of exploration, the joy of discovery, the wonder of the beauty of the world, gratitude for travel opportunities, confidence in safety and protection during the journey, and anticipation for the unforgettable memories you will create. Feel these emotions filling your body and vibrating in every cell of your being as you think about your trip, as you visualize your experiences, as you practice your affirmations. Positive emotions raise your vibrational frequency, attuning your journey to the energy of magic and adventure, and strengthening your ability to manifest these qualities in your reality.

Open yourself to Synchronicity and the Magic of Travel: Synchronicity and magic are essential ingredients of memorable journeys. Open yourself to the possibility of synchronicities and magical moments happening during your trip, trusting that the universe is conspiring to guide you to the right experiences, to divine encounters, to unexpected opportunities, and to perfect moments. Be aware of the signs, coincidences, intuitive impulses, and messages that appear along the way. Follow your intuition, be flexible in your plans, be open to unexpected detours and twists, and allow yourself to be surprised by the magic of travel.

Connect with Local Culture and the Wisdom of Places: A memorable journey is enriched by connecting with the local culture and the wisdom of the places you visit. Immerse yourself in the local culture, try authentic cuisine, learn a few words and phrases in the local language, interact with locals with respect and curiosity, participate in cultural activities and local traditions. Connect with the energy and history of the places you visit, explore ancient temples, historical monuments, sacred natural sites, places with spiritual and cultural significance. Openness to local culture and the wisdom of places enriches your travel experience and expands your consciousness.

Explore Nature and the Beauty of the World: Nature and the beauty of the world are inexhaustible sources of inspiration, revitalization, and spiritual connection during travel. Take time to explore nature at your travel destinations, visit natural parks, paradise beaches, majestic mountains, lush forests, mysterious deserts, serene lakes, flowing rivers, imposing waterfalls, etc. Contemplate the beauty of nature, admire the grandeur of the landscapes, breathe the fresh air, feel the vital energy of the earth, and allow nature to revitalize you, inspire you, and reconnect you with your essence.

Practice Mindfulness and Presence in Each Moment of the Journey: Mindfulness and conscious presence are essential to fully savor each moment of the journey and create lasting memories. Be present in every experience, in every landscape, in every interaction, in every sensation, in every emotion, in every moment of your journey. Disconnect from technological distractions, abandon worries about the past and future, and immerse yourself completely in the present moment. Observe with curiosity and admiration, savor with all your senses, appreciate the beauty of details, and record memories in your heart and mind with mindfulness and conscious presence.

Open yourself to Personal Transformation and Inner Growth Through Travel: Be open to the personal transformation and inner growth that magical journeys and memorable experiences can provide. Allow the journey to challenge you, inspire you, question you, expand you, and transform you. Step out of your comfort zone, face your fears, overcome your limits, learn from new cultures and perspectives, question your beliefs and assumptions, and open yourself to the wisdom that the journey has to offer. Transformative journeys are catalysts for personal growth and expansion of consciousness.

Express Gratitude and Appreciation for Every Travel Experience: Gratitude and appreciation amplify the magic and beauty of memorable journeys. Express gratitude for each experience, for each landscape, for each encounter, for each moment of joy, for each challenge overcome, for each lesson learned, for each synchronicity witnessed, for each memory created. Recognize and appreciate the richness and beauty of your journey, celebrate each precious moment, and record the memories in your heart with deep gratitude and appreciation.

Practices for Co-creating Magical Journeys and Memorable Experiences:

To integrate the principles of conscious co-creation into your magical journeys and memorable experiences, try the following practices:

Meditation on the Magical and Memorable Journey: Set aside daily time for meditation on the magical and memorable journey. Sit in silence, take a deep breath, and visualize yourself embarking on your dream trip, experiencing magical moments, exploring incredible places, connecting with inspiring people, and creating unforgettable memories. Repeat affirmations of magical journeys and memorable experiences during meditation, and feel the thrill of adventure, enthusiasm, and joy filling your heart.

Magical and Memorable Journey Journal: Keep a journal of the magical and memorable journey, where you record your intentions, visualizations, affirmations, synchronicities, magical moments, memorable experiences, insights, lessons learned, and expressions of gratitude throughout your travel journey. Write down the details that make your trip special, the emotions you feel, the memories you create, and the transformations you experience. The magical journey journal becomes a treasure trove of precious memories and a testament to the power of conscious co-creation in your adventures.

Magical and Memorable Journey Vision Map: Create a vision map of the magical and memorable journey, a visual panel that represents your dream trip, the experiences you want to have, the places you want to explore, the people you long to meet, and the memories you want to create. Paste images, phrases, words, symbols, colors, and objects that represent the magic, adventure, beauty, discovery, transformation, connection, joy, and unforgettable memories you want to manifest on your trip. Place your vision map in a visible location and be inspired by it daily, visualizing yourself living the magical and memorable journey you are co-creating.

Travel Gratitude Lists: Create travel gratitude lists before, during, and after your journey. Before your trip, make a list of everything you are already grateful for in advance for your trip, for the opportunities, experiences, memories, synchronicities, magic, and transformation you will experience. During the trip, make daily gratitude lists for each precious moment, for each enriching experience, for each inspiring encounter, for each breathtaking landscape, for each synchronicity witnessed. After the trip, make a final gratitude list for the entire journey, for the unforgettable memories, the transformative lessons, and the magic that the trip brought into your life.

Share Travel Intentions and Experiences with a Co-creation Partner: If you are traveling with a partner, friend, or family member, share your intentions to co-create a magical and memorable trip with your travel companion. Talk about your ideal travel visions, share your expectations, inspire each other to open up to magic and synchronicity, and celebrate together the memorable experiences you co-create along the way. Partner co-creation can amplify the magic and joy of travel, making it even more special and enriching for everyone involved.

Co-creating magical journeys and memorable experiences is about transforming your adventures into soul journeys, opportunities for personal growth, expansion of consciousness, connection with the beauty of the world, and creating precious memories for life. By applying the principles of conscious co-creation to your travels, setting clear intentions, visualizing magic, using empowering affirmations, cultivating positive emotions, opening yourself to synchronicity, connecting with local culture and nature, practicing mindfulness, and expressing gratitude, you can transform your travels into truly transformative adventures, journeys filled with magical moments, inspiring encounters, and unforgettable experiences that nourish your soul and expand your horizons. Start co-creating your magical journeys and memorable experiences today, and prepare to explore the world with eyes of wonder, an open heart, and an adventurous soul!

Chapter 26
Unlocking Creative Potential

Creativity and innovation are the driving forces of human evolution, allowing us to solve challenges, conceive new ideas, and transform our reality in a unique and impactful way. Far from being a privilege of a few, creative potential is an innate ability present in everyone, waiting to be awakened, nurtured, and consciously directed. By understanding and applying the principles of conscious co-creation, it becomes possible to unleash this capacity, promoting original and innovative solutions in various areas of personal, professional, and collective life.

Often, we limit ourselves to conventional approaches and standardized solutions, forgetting the power of creativity and innovation to transform our reality. The good news is that creative solutions and innovation can be consciously co-created, just like any other area of our experience. By applying the principles of conscious co-creation to the domain of creativity, we can unlock our innate creative potential, generate original and innovative ideas, and manifest creative solutions to the challenges we face in our personal, professional, and collective lives.

Creativity as a Vital Force of Consciousness: Expressing Divine Originality

It is important to understand that creativity is a vital force of consciousness, an expression of our divine nature, a manifestation of originality, spontaneity, and the infinity of the universe through us. Creativity is not limited to the arts or areas considered "creative", but permeates all areas of life, from solving everyday problems to scientific, technological, social, artistic, or spiritual innovation. In essence, we are all creative beings, with the innate ability to generate original ideas, find innovative solutions, and express our uniqueness in the world.

Conscious co-creation of creative solutions and innovation is, therefore, a process of connecting with our inner source of creativity, freeing ourselves from the mental and emotional blocks that inhibit our creative potential, aligning ourselves with the energy of inspiration, and allowing for innovative ideas to flow freely through us. It is a process of awakening the creative genius that resides within you, of trusting in your innate ability to generate original solutions, and of consciously collaborating with the creative intelligence of the universe.

Principles for Co-creating Creative Solutions and Innovation

To co-create creative solutions and innovation in any area of your life, you can apply the following principles of conscious co-creation:

Clear Intention for the Creative Solution and Innovation: Start by setting clear and specific intentions for the creative solution and innovation you want to co-create. Ask yourself: "What kind of creative solution do I want to manifest? What kind of problem do I want to solve in an innovative way? What kind of original idea do I want to generate? What kind of creative impact do I want to have on the world? What kind of innovation do I want to co-create?" Set clear and specific intentions, focusing on the quality of originality, innovation, effectiveness, beauty, and positive impact that you want your creative solution to manifest.

Visualize Creative and Innovative Solutions: Use creative visualization to project vivid and detailed images of the creative and innovative solutions you want to manifest. Visualize the solution emerging clearly and completely in your mind, imagine the details, the mechanisms, the results, the positive impact your solution will generate. Visualize yourself having creative insights, connecting ideas in an original way, discovering unexpected solutions, experiencing moments of "Eureka!" and divine inspiration. Engage all your senses in visualization, seeing, hearing, feeling, smelling, and tasting the experience of co-creating creative solutions and innovation.

Affirmations for Creativity and Innovation: Use positive and empowering affirmations to program your subconscious mind with beliefs about creativity, innovation, and genius. Examples of affirmations: "I co-create creative and innovative solutions with ease and joy," "I am a channel for divine creativity and original innovation," "Creative and innovative ideas flow freely through me," "I am naturally creative and resourceful,"

"I find innovative solutions to all the challenges I face," "I am grateful for my innate creativity and my ability to innovate." Repeat these affirmations daily, with conviction and positive emotion, to strengthen your mental projection.

Cultivate Positive Emotions of Inspiration, Curiosity, and Creative Enthusiasm: Seek to cultivate and maintain positive emotions associated with inspiration, curiosity, and creative enthusiasm, such as joy, passion, excitement, wonder, fascination, contentment, freedom, lightness, and spontaneity. Feel these emotions filling your body and vibrating in every cell of your being as you engage in creative activities, as you seek innovative solutions, as you explore new ideas, as you connect with your inner source of creativity. Positive emotions raise your vibrational frequency, attuning your mind to the energy of creativity and innovation, and strengthening your ability to generate original ideas.

Silence the Critical Mind and Open Up to the Creative Flow: The critical mind, judgment, self-censorship, and fear of failure are the greatest enemies of creativity. Silence the critical mind, learn to observe your thoughts without judgment, and open yourself to the creative flow of your intuition, your imagination, and your spontaneity. Allow yourself to explore ideas without censorship, even those that seem strange, absurd, or "outside the box." Free yourself from the need for perfection, the fear of making mistakes or being criticized, and trust your ability to generate original ideas, even if they are not perfect at first glance.

Creative flow flourishes in the absence of judgment and the freedom of experimentation.

Stimulate Curiosity, Exploration, and Experimentation: Creativity is fueled by curiosity, exploration, and experimentation. Cultivate your innate curiosity, question things, ask questions, explore new areas of knowledge, be interested in diverse subjects, challenge your own beliefs and assumptions. Try new approaches, new techniques, new tools, new perspectives, new ways of doing things. Explore different fields of creativity, from visual arts to music, writing, dance, theater, cooking, gardening, science, technology, social innovation, etc. Curiosity, exploration, and experimentation expand your mind, enrich your creative repertoire, and open doors to innovation.

Connect with the Inspiration of Nature and Art: Nature and art are inexhaustible sources of creative inspiration. Connect with nature, observe the beauty, complexity, diversity, and harmony of natural ecosystems, be inspired by the shapes, colors, patterns, sounds, and rhythms of nature. Expose yourself to art in all its forms, visit museums, art galleries, concerts, plays, dance performances, films, read books, listen to music, appreciate the beauty and expressiveness of works of art created by others. Nature and art nourish the creative soul, awaken the imagination, and inspire the generation of new ideas.

Practice Brainstorming, Mind Mapping, and Other Creative Techniques: Use brainstorming, mind mapping, and other creative tools to stimulate the generation of ideas, the connection of concepts, the exploration of innovative solutions, and the organization of creative thinking. Brainstorming allows you to generate a large number of ideas freely, without judgment, stimulating the free association of concepts and the creative explosion. Mind mapping helps to organize ideas in a visual and hierarchical way, facilitating the identification of patterns, connections, and new perspectives. Explore different creative techniques and discover the ones that best suit your thinking style and your creative processes.

Create a Creative and Inspiring Environment: The physical and mental environment profoundly influences creativity. Create a creative and inspiring environment around you, both in your workspace and in your home. Organize your workspace in a way that promotes concentration, fluidity, and inspiration. Decorate the environment with vibrant colors, inspiring objects, works of art, plants, natural light, and elements that motivate you and stimulate your creativity. Minimize distractions, noise, and clutter, creating a space that encourages concentration, introspection, and creative flow.

Collaborate with Collective Creativity and Constructive Feedback: Creativity is not an isolated process, but it also flourishes in collaboration and interaction with others. Share your ideas with other people, seek constructive feedback, participate in group brainstorms, collaborate on creative projects, join creative communities. The diversity of perspectives, the exchange of ideas, constructive feedback, and the energy of collective collaboration can amplify your creativity, generate more innovative solutions, and enrich your creative process.

Practices for Co-creating Creative Solutions and Innovation:

To integrate the principles of conscious co-creation into your journey of generating creative solutions and innovation, try the following practices:

Creative Inspiration Meditation: Set aside regular time for creative inspiration meditation. Sit in silence, take a deep breath, and visualize yourself connecting to the universal source of divine creativity, diving into an ocean of innovative ideas, opening yourself to the inspiration that flows freely through you. Repeat affirmations of creativity and innovation during meditation, and feel the thrill of inspiration and creative enthusiasm filling your heart.

Journal of Creativity and Innovation: Keep a journal of creativity and innovation, where you record your creative ideas, your innovative insights, your moments of inspiration, your creative challenges, your original solutions, your creative experiments, and your learning in the creative process. Write down the ideas that arise spontaneously, the insights that illuminate you, the creative dreams that visit you, the innovative solutions you find, and the reflections on your creative process. The creativity journal becomes a repository of original ideas and a guide for your creative development.

Conscious Creative Brainstorming Sessions: Schedule conscious creative brainstorming sessions to explore a specific problem, generate innovative ideas, or develop creative solutions. Set a limited time for the brainstorming session, invite others to participate, create a relaxed and inspiring environment, and follow the rules of brainstorming: generate as many ideas as possible, without judgment, without criticism, encouraging the free association of concepts and exploring "crazy" or "outside the box" ideas. Record all ideas generated during the brainstorming session, and then select and refine the most promising ideas to develop creative and innovative solutions.

Inspiring Creative Walks in Nature: Take inspiring creative walks in nature to stimulate your creative mind and connect with nature's source of inspiration. Walk in parks, gardens, forests, beaches, or other natural environments that inspire you, observing the beauty, diversity, and harmony of nature with mindfulness. Let nature revitalize you, inspire you, and connect you with your innate creativity. Take a notebook and pen with you to write down creative ideas, innovative insights, and inspirations that arise during the creative walk in nature.

Weekly Creative Challenges: Set yourself weekly creative challenges to stimulate your creative mind and expand your potential for innovation. Choose a different creative challenge each week, such as "creating a new recipe," "writing a poem or song," "painting or drawing something original," "creating a prototype of a new product or service," "solving a complex problem in an innovative way," "organizing a creative event," etc. Embrace creative challenges with enthusiasm and curiosity, have fun in the creative process, and celebrate your creative achievements at the end of each week.

Co-creating creative solutions and innovation is about awakening the creative genius that resides within you, unleashing your innovative potential, and transforming your ability to solve problems and generate original ideas in all areas of your life. By applying the principles of conscious co-creation to your creative journey, setting clear intentions, visualizing innovative solutions, using empowering affirmations, cultivating positive emotions, silencing the critical mind, stimulating curiosity, connecting with the inspiration of nature and art, practicing creative techniques, and creating a creative environment, you can unlock your innate creative potential, generate original and innovative solutions, and manifest a significant creative impact in the world. Start co-creating creative solutions and innovation today, and prepare to witness the flourishing of your creative genius and the magic of innovation manifesting in your reality!

Chapter 27
Co-creating the Manifestation of Dreams

Co-creating the manifestation of specific dreams is a conscious process that combines intention, energetic alignment, and inspired action to transform deep desires into tangible reality. Each goal, whether material, professional, relational, or personal, can be achieved by refining the clarity of intention, overcoming limiting beliefs, and applying advanced visualization and affirmation techniques. By mastering these principles and integrating manifestation into the natural flow of life, it becomes possible to attract and concretize with precision that which truly resonates with your essence.

Often, we have deep dreams and desires, but we feel that their fulfillment is out of reach, dependent on external factors or luck. The good news is that the manifestation of specific dreams can be consciously co-created, with intention, focus, persistence, and mastery of advanced techniques. By learning to refine our intention, overcome internal and external obstacles, accelerate the manifestation process, and maintain energetic alignment with our dream, we can become masters of conscious manifestation, capable of realizing the goals that truly resonate with our soul.

The Manifestation of Specific Dreams as Art and Science: Combining Intention and Technique

It is important to understand that the manifestation of specific dreams is both an art and a science. It is an art because it requires intuition, creativity, energetic sensitivity, faith, and surrender to the flow of life. It is a science because it is based on universal principles, laws of the mind and the universe, specific techniques, and consistent practices. Mastering the art of manifesting specific dreams implies combining intuition and technique, inspiration and discipline, faith and action, surrender and intention, creating a powerful synergy that drives the achievement of your goals.

The conscious co-creation of the manifestation of specific dreams is, therefore, a process of focused intention, energetic alignment, overcoming resistance, inspired action, and cultivating faith and gratitude. It is a process of becoming a master of your own reality, capable of using the tools of the mind and the universe to transform your deepest dreams into tangible reality.

Advanced Principles and Techniques to Co-create the Manifestation of Specific Dreams:

To co-create the manifestation of specific dreams and achieve concrete goals, we can apply the following principles and advanced techniques of conscious co-creation:

Specific, Clear, and Emotionally Charged Intention: The first crucial step to manifesting a specific dream is to define a clear, specific, and emotionally charged intention. It is not enough to have a vague desire or a generic goal; it is necessary to clarify exactly what you want to manifest, with as much detail as possible, and connect emotionally with the realization of that dream, feeling the joy, enthusiasm, gratitude, and fulfillment as if your dream were already a present reality. The more specific, clear, and emotionally charged your intention is, the more powerful your mental projection will be and the faster the manifestation will be.

Detailed and Multisensory Visualization of the Realized Dream: Detailed and multisensory visualization is an advanced manifestation technique that amplifies the power of your intention. Don't just visualize your dream as a static or abstract image; create a vivid and detailed scene of your dream already realized, involving all your senses in the visualization. See yourself enjoying your dream, hear the sounds of the environment, feel the physical sensations, smell the aromas, savor the details of the experience. The richer, more detailed, and multisensory your visualization is, the more powerful and effective your mental projection will be.

Powerful and Personalized Affirmations for the Specific Dream: Powerful and personalized affirmations are essential tools to program your subconscious mind with beliefs of achievement and to strengthen your intention to manifest. Use specific affirmations focused on your concrete dream, formulated in a positive way, in the present tense, and emotionally charged. Examples of affirmations: "I manifest [my specific dream] with ease and joy", "I am the creator of my reality and I manifest [my specific dream] now", "I vibrate in the frequency of the realization of [my specific dream]", "I am grateful for having already manifested [my specific dream] in my reality", "I deserve and receive [my specific dream] now and always". Repeat these affirmations daily, with conviction and positive emotion, to reprogram your subconscious mind and strengthen your mental projection.

Creative Scripting and the "Story of the Realized Dream": Creative scripting is an advanced technique that consists of writing the "story of your dream already realized", as if it were a movie script or a literary tale. Describe in detail what your life, your emotions, your experiences, your sensations, your relationships, your environment, your daily routine, and all aspects of your reality would be like after the manifestation of your dream. Write in the present tense, with vivid emotion and detail, as if you were living the reality of your dream at this very moment. Read your creative script daily, feeling grateful and excited for the reality of your dream already manifested. Creative scripting helps to anchor your intention in the mental and emotional plane, strengthening your manifestation projection.

Detailed Vision Maps Focused on the Specific Dream: The vision map, which we have already explored in previous chapters, can be an even more powerful tool when focused on the manifestation of a specific dream. Create a vision map dedicated exclusively to your concrete dream, gathering images, phrases, words, symbols and objects that represent the reality of your dream already manifested in all its details. Divide the vision map into specific areas of your dream, such as material, relational, emotional, professional, personal aspects, etc., and fill each area with vivid and inspiring details. Place your vision map in a visible location and be inspired by it daily, visualizing yourself living the reality of the dream you are co-creating.

Augmented Senses and Mental Virtual Reality Technique: The augmented senses technique consists of intensifying the sensory experience of visualization, using all the senses in a vivid and realistic way. When visualizing your dream come true, not only see the images in your mind, but increase the intensity of the sensations, imagining more vibrant colors, clearer sounds, more intense smells, more delicious flavors and more palpable textures. Create a "mental virtual reality" of your dream, making the visualization experience as real and immersive as possible. The more vivid and sensory your visualization is, the more powerful its impact on physical reality will be.

Overcoming Limiting Beliefs and Specific Internal Resistances: To manifest specific dreams, it is essential to identify and overcome the limiting beliefs and internal resistances that may be sabotaging the realization of your goal. Ask yourself: "What are my fears and doubts about the realization of this dream? What are the negative beliefs I have about the possibility of achieving this goal? What are the internal resistances that prevent me from moving forward with confidence and faith towards my dream?". Use the techniques for releasing limiting beliefs that we explored in Chapter 10 to dismantle these specific negative beliefs and internal resistances, replacing them with empowering beliefs and affirmations of self-confidence and self-worth.

Accelerating Manifestation with Emotional Release Techniques (EFT, Ho'oponopono, Sedona Method): Emotional release techniques, such as Emotional Freedom Techniques (EFT), Ho'oponopono and Sedona Method, can be powerful tools to accelerate the process of manifesting specific dreams, releasing emotional blocks, internal resistances and stagnant energies that may be delaying the realization of your goal. Explore these emotional release techniques, learn to use them effectively, and apply them regularly to clear the energetic path to the manifestation of your dream, removing obstacles and allowing the energy of fulfillment to flow freely into your life.

Inspired Action Aligned with the Specific Dream: The manifestation of specific dreams does not happen only on the mental and energetic plane; it requires inspired action aligned with your goal. Be attentive to the impulses of inspired action that arise from your intuition, your heart and your inner wisdom, and follow those impulses with confidence and enthusiasm. Take small, practical, and consistent steps toward your dream, even if the full path is not entirely clear at first. Look for opportunities, resources, contacts, and information that can bring you closer to your goal. Inspired action is the engine that drives the manifestation of your specific dreams into physical reality.

Intelligent Surrender to the Divine Flow and Trust in Perfect Timing: While focused intention and inspired action are essential, the manifestation of specific dreams also requires intelligent surrender to the divine flow and trust in the perfect timing of the universe. Release excessive attachment to the outcome and the need to control every detail of the manifestation process. Trust that the universe is conspiring in your favor to guide you to the realization of your dream, at the perfect time and in the most appropriate way. Allow yourself to flow with the natural rhythm of life, accept unexpected twists and turns, trust in the wisdom of the universe, and maintain unwavering faith that your dream is manifesting, even if it is not yet visible on the physical plane.

Celebrating Small Achievements and Expressing Continuous Gratitude: Throughout the journey of manifesting specific dreams, it is essential to celebrate small achievements and express continuous gratitude for each step, for each progress, for each synchronicity, for each opportunity, for each blessing that arises on the path to achieving your goal. Recognize and appreciate the signs that your dream is manifesting, even if they are small and subtle. Gratitude amplifies the energy of manifestation, attracts more blessings into your life, and strengthens your faith and trust in the process of conscious co-creation.

Advanced Practices to Co-create the Manifestation of Specific Dreams:

To integrate the principles and advanced techniques of conscious co-creation into your journey of manifesting specific dreams, try the following practices:

Specific Dream Manifestation Meditation: Set aside daily time for specific dream manifestation meditation. Sit in silence, breathe deeply and visualize yourself living the reality of your dream already manifested, using the augmented senses and mental virtual reality technique. Repeat powerful and personalized affirmations for your specific dream during meditation, and feel the emotion of fulfillment, joy and gratitude filling your heart.

Intensive Creative Scripting Sessions: Schedule intensive creative scripting sessions to write the "story of your dream come true" in a detailed, vivid and emotionally charged way. Dedicate time and energy to immerse yourself in writing your creative script, exploring all aspects of the reality of your dream already manifested, and allowing the emotion of fulfillment to fill you completely. Read your creative script aloud, with conviction and enthusiasm, feeling grateful and excited for the reality of your dream already manifested.

Creating a Specific Dream Manifestation Altar: Create a specific dream manifestation altar, a sacred space dedicated exclusively to the manifestation of your specific goal. Place on the altar your detailed vision map, symbolic objects that represent your dream, crystals that amplify the energy of manifestation, incense, candles, flowers, and other elements that resonate with your intention. Dedicate time daily to your manifestation altar, meditating, visualizing, affirming, writing in your manifestation journal, and connecting with the energy of fulfilling your dream.

Daily Emotional Release Techniques (EFT, Ho'oponopono, Sedona Method): Incorporate emotional release techniques into your daily routine, taking time to practice EFT, Ho'oponopono or the Sedona Method to release emotional blocks, internal resistances and stagnant energies that may be delaying the manifestation of your specific dream. Use these techniques whenever you feel fears, doubts, insecurities, limiting beliefs or negative emotions that may be sabotaging your manifestation journey.

Specific Dream Manifestation Partner and Goal Achievement Mastermind: Find a specific dream manifestation partner or join a goal achievement mastermind group to share your intentions, your progress, your challenges, your learnings, and to receive and offer support, encouragement, feedback and creative brainstorming. The collective energy, shared wisdom and mutual support of a mastermind group can amplify your ability to co-create the manifestation of specific dreams and accelerate the achievement of your goals.

Co-creating the manifestation of specific dreams is mastering the art of conscious projection at an advanced level, becoming a master of your own reality and realizing the goals that truly resonate with your soul. By applying the principles and advanced techniques of conscious co-creation to the manifestation of specific dreams, by refining your intention, by visualizing with details, by using powerful affirmations, by writing creative scripts, by creating focused vision maps, by using emotional release techniques, by following inspired action, by surrendering to the divine flow, and by celebrating small achievements with gratitude, you can transform your deepest dreams into tangible reality, manifest the goals your heart desires, and live a life full of fulfillment, purpose, and joy. Start today to co-create the manifestation of your specific dreams, and prepare to witness the magic of transforming your vision into concrete reality!

Chapter 28
Co-creating Beyond the Individual

Co-creation goes beyond the individual sphere and is exponentially strengthened when carried out in community, directed towards the greater good. When people come together with aligned intentions and shared purpose, they form a powerful energy field capable of generating significant changes in society. By cultivating cooperation, harmony, and collective vision, it becomes possible to manifest more just, sustainable, and prosperous realities, benefiting not only those involved but all of humanity.

Often, we focus on our individual goals and desires, forgetting the power of unity and collaboration to create a better world for all. The good news is that co-creating in community and for the greater good is a real and accessible possibility, through the conscious application of the principles of collective co-creation. By learning to align our intentions with those of others, to cultivate harmony and cooperation in groups, to project shared visions, and to act together for a greater purpose, we can become conscious co-creators of a more positive and prosperous future for all mankind.

Collective Co-creation as a Force for Global Transformation: Uniting Intentions for the Common Good

It is essential to understand that the collective consciousness of humanity is a powerful force that shapes the reality of our world. Our collective thoughts, beliefs, intentions, and emotions, when consciously directed towards the greater good, have the power to transform our societies, our communities, our planet, and our future. Collective co-creation is not a distant utopia, but rather an emerging reality, driven by the growing awareness of the interconnection, interdependence, and shared responsibility that unites us as human beings.

Conscious co-creation in community and for the greater good is, therefore, a process of aligning collective intentions, cultivating harmony and cooperation in groups, projecting shared visions for a better future, and taking joint and inspired action to manifest that desired future. It is a process of awakening to our power as collective co-creators, of joining forces for the common good, and of building a more just, peaceful, sustainable, prosperous, and harmonious world for all beings.

Principles and Strategies for Co-creating in Community and for the Greater Good:

To co-create in community and for the greater good, manifesting positive changes on a large scale, we can apply the following principles and strategies of conscious collective co-creation:

Clear Collective Intention Aligned with the Greater Good: The first essential step for effective collective co-creation is to define a clear collective intention aligned with the greater good of all involved and the wider community. It is not enough to have a group of people gathered together; the group needs to consciously define a common purpose, a shared vision, a collective goal that benefits everyone and that resonates with universal values such as peace, justice, harmony, sustainability, prosperity, health, and well-being. The clearer, more aligned, and focused on the greater good the collective intention is, the more powerful the group's co-creation will be.

Cultivating Harmony, Cooperation, and Conscious Communication in the Group: Harmony, cooperation, and conscious communication are fundamental to the success of collective co-creation. It is necessary to cultivate an environment of respect, trust, empathy, active listening, open dialogue, genuine collaboration, and peaceful conflict resolution within the group. Promote diversity of perspectives, value the contributions of each member, celebrate individual and collective talents, and build positive synergy that strengthens the energy and effectiveness of the group's co-creation. Harmony, cooperation, and conscious communication create the foundation for powerful and transformative collective co-creation.

Collective and Shared Visualization of the Desired Reality for the Greater Good: Collective and shared visualization amplifies the power of the group's intention and strengthens the mental projection of the desired reality for the greater good. Conduct guided group visualization sessions where all members together imagine the reality they wish to co-create for the community, society, or the planet. Use vivid and detailed images, involving all the senses in the visualization, and synchronize the positive emotions of the group in the frequency of the realization of the shared vision. Collective and shared visualization creates a powerful energy field that drives the manifestation of the desired reality on a large scale.

Collective and Unified Affirmations for the Greater Good: Use collective and unified affirmations to program the subconscious mind of the group and strengthen the mental projection of the desired reality for the greater good. Create specific affirmations focused on the collective intention, formulated in a positive way, in the present tense, and emotionally charged, that resonate with the shared values and goals of the group. Examples of collective affirmations: "We co-create a world of peace, justice and harmony for all", "Our community flourishes in prosperity, health and well-being", "We manifest sustainable and innovative solutions to the challenges of our planet", "We are conscious co-creators of a better future for humanity", "We vibrate in the frequency of love, compassion and unity, manifesting the greater good for all beings". Repeat these affirmations in a group regularly, with conviction and positive emotion, to strengthen your collective mental projection.

Creating Symbols, Rituals, and Collective Co-creation Practices: Creating symbols, rituals, and collective co-creation practices strengthens group identity, internal cohesion, and the energy of collective manifestation. Develop visual, sound, or gestural symbols that represent the collective intention and shared vision of the group. Create rituals of connection, alignment of intentions, collective visualization, unified affirmations, and celebration of the group's progress and achievements. Incorporate regular practices of group meditation, collective creative brainstorming, shared mind mapping, and other collective co-creation techniques that resonate with the energy and purpose of the group. Collective symbols, rituals, and practices strengthen the group bond and amplify the power of collective co-creation.

Inspired Collective Action Aligned with the Greater Good: Collective co-creation is not limited to the mental and energetic plane; it requires inspired collective action aligned with the group's shared intention and vision. Be attentive to the impulses of inspired action that arise from collective intuition, group wisdom, and the inner guidance of each member, and follow those impulses with courage, enthusiasm, and collaboration. Define concrete and realistic action plans, distribute tasks and responsibilities, coordinate efforts, and move forward together towards the manifestation of the desired reality for the greater good. Inspired collective action is the engine that drives the transformation of shared vision into tangible reality in the world.

Serving and Empowering Leadership in Collective Co-creation: Serving and empowering leadership is essential to guide and facilitate the process of collective co-creation effectively and harmoniously. The servant leader is not an authoritarian boss, but rather a facilitator, a catalyst, an inspirer, a connector, and a servant of the group. The servant leader actively listens to the needs and visions of each member, promotes the participation and empowerment of all, facilitates communication and collaboration, manages conflicts in a peaceful and constructive way, and guides the group with wisdom, integrity, and compassion towards the realization of the collective intention. Serving and empowering leadership strengthens group cohesion, maximizes collective creative potential, and ensures that collective co-creation is an inclusive, participatory, and beneficial process for all.

Connecting with Conscious Co-creation Networks and Communities: To expand the impact of collective co-creation and strengthen your own practice, it is important to connect with conscious co-creation networks and communities that share similar values, purposes, and intentions. Participate in meetings, events, workshops, webinars, online platforms, and social networks dedicated to conscious collective co-creation, exchange experiences, share knowledge, collaborate on joint projects, and build alliances and partnerships with other conscious co-creators. Connecting with conscious co-creation networks and communities broadens your perspective, strengthens your motivation, expands your reach, and multiplies the impact of your collective co-creation.

Focusing on the Greater Good and Contributing to the World: The fundamental principle of co-creation in community is to focus on the greater good and positive contribution to the world. Make sure that the collective intention, the group's actions, and the results of co-creation are always aligned with ethical values, universal principles, and the well-being of all beings. Seek to create solutions that benefit not only the group but also the wider community, society, the planet, and future generations. Conscious co-creation in community is an opportunity to transcend individual and egoic interests and to contribute significantly to building a better world for all.

Celebrating Collective Progress and Expressing Gratitude for Co-creation in Community: Throughout the journey of collective co-creation, it is essential to celebrate the group's progress and achievements and express gratitude for the opportunity to co-create in community and for the greater good. Recognize and appreciate the efforts of each member, celebrate milestones achieved, share successes, and express gratitude for the energy, wisdom, and power of collective co-creation. Celebration and gratitude strengthen the spirit of unity, group motivation, and the energy of collective manifestation, driving the continued co-creation of positive change on a large scale.

Practices for Co-creating in Community and for the Greater Good:

To integrate the principles and strategies of conscious collective co-creation into your community initiatives and greater good projects, try the following practices:

Collective Intention Alignment Meetings: Organize regular collective intention alignment meetings with your group or community. Use these meetings to clarify and refine the collective intention, to discuss and resolve challenges, to share progress, to inspire and motivate members, and to strengthen the bond and cohesion of the group. Incorporate group meditation practices, collective visualization, unified affirmations, and collective creative brainstorming into collective intention alignment meetings.

Creating a Virtual or Physical "Collective Sacred Space": Create a "collective sacred space" for your group, whether virtual (such as an online group dedicated to collective co-creation) or physical (such as a regular meeting place for group activities). Use this collective sacred space for meetings, for collective co-creation practices, for sharing experiences, for mutual support, and for celebrating the group's achievements.

Co-creating in community and for the greater good is an act of conscious participation in the evolution of our world. By uniting our intentions, our actions, and our energy with others who share similar values and aspirations, we can co-create a more just, peaceful, sustainable, and prosperous reality for all beings.

Chapter 29
Habits and Continuous Practices

Maintaining conscious co-creation as an integral part of life requires a continuous commitment to practices and habits that support the expansion of consciousness and intentional manifestation. More than a technique, it is a lifestyle that is consolidated through the disciplined repetition of daily rituals, mental and emotional alignment, and an attitude of presence and gratitude. By integrating co-creation into all areas of existence, it becomes a natural flow, allowing each daily experience to reinforce the mastery of manifestation and the power of conscious intention.

Often, we start personal development practices with enthusiasm and motivation, but over time, routine, challenges, and the distractions of everyday life can cause these practices to dilute, get lost, or become sporadic. The good news is that maintaining conscious co-creation throughout life is possible and rewarding, through the consolidation of habits and continuous practices that reinforce your mastery of conscious projection and that sustain the transformation of your reality in a consistent and lasting way. By creating a routine of conscious co-creation practices, by cultivating mental, emotional, and behavioral habits that resonate with the principles of conscious projection, and by integrating conscious co-creation into all areas of our lives, we can keep the flame of co-creation alive, expand our potential for manifestation and live an increasingly full life, conscious and aligned with our deepest dreams.

Conscious Co-creation as a Lifestyle: A Continuous Commitment to the Expansion of Consciousness

It is important to understand that conscious co-creation is not a final destination to be reached, but rather a continuous journey of expansion of consciousness, self-improvement, personal growth, and manifestation of our desired reality. Maintaining conscious co-creation throughout life is, therefore, a continuous commitment to this journey, a persistent dedication to the practice, learning, evolution, and integration of the principles of conscious projection in all dimensions of our experience. It is a commitment to consciously live as co-creators of our reality, to take responsibility for our power of projection, and to use that power wisely, intentionally, and in alignment with the greater good.

Continuous Habits and Practices to Maintain Conscious Co-creation Throughout Life:

To maintain conscious co-creation as a permanent lifestyle, supporting your mastery of conscious projection throughout your journey, we can incorporate the following continuous habits and practices into our daily and weekly routines:

Daily Meditation of Conscious Co-creation: A Morning Ritual of Alignment: Daily meditation of conscious co-creation is a fundamental habit to keep the flame of conscious projection alive throughout life. Set aside a specific time each morning, ideally upon waking, to practice conscious co-creation meditation. Use different meditation techniques that we explore throughout the book, such as visualization meditation, affirmation meditation, gratitude meditation, emotional release meditation, creative inspiration meditation, etc. Vary your meditations, explore new approaches, and maintain the practice of daily meditation as a morning ritual of alignment, which connects you with your intention to consciously co-create your reality throughout the day.

Conscious Daily Review of Thoughts and Beliefs: A Guardian of the Mind: Conscious daily review of thoughts and beliefs is an essential habit to keep your mind aligned with the frequency of conscious co-creation. Take a few moments throughout the day, especially before starting important or challenging activities, to consciously observe your thoughts and beliefs. Identify negative, limiting, or misaligned thoughts with your goals and values, and apply the techniques for transforming limiting beliefs that we explored in Chapter 10 to dismantle these negative beliefs and replace them with empowering beliefs and positive affirmations. Transform the conscious daily review of thoughts and beliefs into a "guardian of the mind", which helps you maintain control over your internal dialogue and direct your mental energy towards conscious co-creation.

Creative Visualization and Affirmations Throughout the Day: Moments of Conscious Projection: Don't just practice visualization and affirmations during your morning meditation; integrate creative visualization and positive affirmations throughout the day, transforming everyday moments into "moments of conscious projection." Visualize the desired reality while waiting in traffic, while walking, while washing dishes, while taking a shower, while waiting in line, etc. Repeat your positive affirmations mentally or in a low voice while getting dressed, while making coffee, while exercising, while waiting for an appointment, etc. Take advantage of the small breaks in your day to practice visualization and affirmations, transforming seemingly banal moments into opportunities to reinforce your conscious projection.

Continuous Gratitude Journal: A Record of Daily Abundance: The continuous gratitude journal is a powerful habit to keep your energy aligned with the frequency of abundance and positivity throughout life. Take a few minutes each night, before bed, to write in your gratitude journal. Record at least 3 to 5 things you are grateful for that day, big or small, material or immaterial, personal or collective. Remember positive moments, achievements, blessings, synchronicities, opportunities, relationships, learning, and everything that made you feel grateful and appreciated throughout the day. The daily practice of gratitude strengthens your abundance mindset, raises your vibrational frequency and attracts more blessings into your life.

Moments of Mindfulness and Conscious Presence: Savoring the Present Moment: Mindfulness and conscious presence are essential habits to fully experience the co-created reality and to stay connected with the power of the present moment. Practice mindfulness in all your daily activities, paying full attention to your sensations, your thoughts, your emotions, the environment around you, the taste of food, the touch of water, the sound of voices, etc. Set aside specific times of the day to practice mindfulness meditation, focusing on the breath, body sensations, sounds, aromas, flavors, or any other object of mindfulness. Mindfulness and conscious presence allow you to fully savor the present moment, reduce stress, increase mental clarity and strengthen your connection with your essence.

Weekly Review of the Co-creation Journey: Reflection, Planning and Adjustment: The weekly review of the co-creation journey is a strategic habit to stay on track, assess progress, identify challenges, plan the next steps and adjust your approach as needed. Set aside a specific time each week, ideally on the weekend, to review your co-creation journey from the past week. Revisit your gratitude journal, review your visualizations and affirmations, reflect on your experiences, identify your successes and challenges, analyze repeating patterns, and plan your intentions, goals, and co-creation practices for the following week. The weekly review allows you to maintain awareness of your co-creation journey, learn from your experiences, and adjust your approach continuously and strategically.

Continuous Learning and Expansion of Consciousness: Nourishing the Mind and Spirit: Conscious co-creation is a journey of continuous learning and expansion of consciousness. Stay open to learning, explore new knowledge, read inspiring books, participate in workshops, webinars, online courses, lectures, events and other activities that expand your understanding of conscious co-creation and related topics such as quantum physics, neuroscience, psychology positive, spirituality, metaphysics, etc. Nourish your mind and spirit with knowledge, wisdom, inspiration, and new perspectives, continuously expanding your awareness and your mastery of co-creation.

Connection with the Community of Conscious Co-creators: Support, Sharing and Mutual Inspiration: Maintaining connection with the community of conscious co-creators is fundamental for support, sharing, mutual inspiration and strengthening your long-term co-creation journey. Keep in touch with your accountability partner, participate in your mastermind group, join online or face-to-face conscious co-creation communities, participate in events and meetings of co-creators, share your experiences, receive support, offer encouragement, exchange ideas, get inspired and motivate each other with others who are following a similar path. The community of conscious co-creators offers a valuable support system to sustain your journey and expand your co-creation potential.

Flexibility, Adaptability and Compassion with Yourself: Dancing with the Flow of Life: The journey of conscious co-creation throughout life is neither linear nor perfect; there will be ups and downs, challenges and achievements, moments of clarity and moments of doubt, periods of great flow and periods of apparent stagnation. It is essential to cultivate flexibility, adaptability and compassion with yourself along the journey. Accept unexpected twists and turns, adapt your practices as needed, forgive yourself for "slips" or difficulties, celebrate small progress, and persist in your practice with love, faith, and determination. Remember that conscious co-creation is a continuous dance with the flow of life, and that mastery of conscious projection is a life journey, not a final destination.

Celebrating Achievements and Expressing Gratitude for the Continuous Journey: Recognizing the Magic of Co-creation in Life: Finally, it is essential to celebrate achievements, big and small, throughout the journey of conscious co-creation, and to express continuous gratitude for the magic of manifestation that manifests in your life, for the blessings you receive, for the transformations you experience, for the personal growth you achieve, and for the joy of living a consciously co-created life. Recognize and appreciate the beauty, abundance, and magic of co-creation that manifests in all areas of your life, and express gratitude for the privilege of being a conscious co-creator of your own reality. Celebration and gratitude amplify the energy of manifestation, strengthen your faith and motivation, and enrich your journey of conscious co-creation throughout life.

Integrating Conscious Co-creation into All Areas of Life:

To maintain conscious co-creation as a permanent lifestyle, it is important to integrate it into all areas of your life, applying the principles of conscious projection in all domains of your experience. From health and well-being, to financial abundance and prosperity, to harmonious home and sacred space, to magical journeys and memorable experiences, to creative solutions and innovation, to the manifestation of specific dreams, to co-creation in community and for the greater good, and to all other areas of your life, consciously apply the principles of co-creation, project clear intentions, visualize the desired reality, use empowering affirmations, cultivate positive emotions, follow inspired action, surrender to the divine flow, and express continuous gratitude. Integrate conscious co-creation into all dimensions of your existence, transforming it into a way of being and living that manifests itself in all moments and in all areas of your experience.

Maintaining conscious co-creation throughout life is embracing a continuous journey of personal growth, expansion of consciousness and manifestation of the reality of your dreams. It is a process of becoming a master of your own life, of consciously living as a co-creator of your experience, and of dancing in harmony with the universe, projecting a reality full of beauty, abundance, joy, purpose and love, in all moments and in all areas of your life. Start today to consolidate the habits and continuous practices of conscious co-creation in your daily routine, and prepare to witness an extraordinary transformation in your life, as you become a master of conscious projection and fully live the reality that you choose to co-create, throughout your entire journey!

Chapter 30
Expansion and New Horizons

The journey of conscious co-creation does not end; it expands, revealing new horizons and unlimited possibilities. Every thought, emotion, and intention shapes reality in a continuous way, inviting the evolution and improvement of conscious manifestation. Mastering co-creation is not an end, but a dynamic process, a constant dance with life. By embracing this expansion, you open yourself to new discoveries, challenges, and opportunities, cultivating an existence full of purpose, creativity, and fulfillment.

It is essential to remember that conscious co-creation is not a final destination, but rather a continuous dance, an evolutionary process and a journey of constant expansion. Reality is in perpetual motion, in constant flux, in incessant transformation. Just like dance, conscious co-creation is a dynamic, fluid and adaptable expression, which adjusts to the rhythms of life, changes in the environment, nuances of emotions and the evolution of consciousness.

Evolution is inherent in the journey of conscious co-creation. As you practice, experiment, learn, reflect and integrate the principles of conscious projection, your understanding of co-creation deepens, your manifestation skills improve, your confidence in your power as a co-creator strengthens, and your ability to consciously live the desired reality expands. Allow yourself to continually evolve on your co-creation journey, embrace new learning, explore new techniques, challenge your own limits, and celebrate each step of your evolutionary journey.

Expansion is the essence of the dance of co-creation. Conscious co-creation invites you to expand your consciousness, broaden your horizons, explore new territories of your mind, heart and spirit, and open yourself to new possibilities and unlimited potential. Expand your vision of reality, question your limiting beliefs, challenge your own expectations, embrace change, explore the unknown, and allow your consciousness to expand beyond the limits of your imagination. The expansion of consciousness is the fuel that feeds the continuous dance of co-creation and that propels you to new horizons of fulfillment and fullness.

As I conclude this book, I invite you to look to the future with enthusiasm, hope and a sense of unlimited potential. The journey of conscious co-creation is a gateway to a universe of infinite possibilities, where your wildest dreams can come true, where your ability to create and manifest is unlimited, and where your life experience can be increasingly fulfilling, meaningful, joyful and abundant.

The new horizons that open up before you are vast and unexplored. Continue to dance with conscious projection, experiment with new techniques, apply the principles of co-creation in new areas of your life, challenge your own limits, expand your consciousness, and discover the unlimited potential that lies within you and in your ability to co-create your reality. Do not settle for the ordinary, the predictable or the limited; dare to dream big, imagine the unimaginable, believe in the impossible, and allow your dance of co-creation to take you to new heights of achievement, abundance and joy, beyond anything you ever imagined possible.

And so, we come to the end of this stage of our exploratory journey of conscious co-creation. But in truth, this is just the beginning of a continuous dance, an endless adventure, a life journey full of magic, potential and possibilities. The dance of co-creation continues, in every thought, in every emotion, in every intention, in every action, in every moment of your life. Now, more than ever, you are aware of your power as a co-creator, empowered with practical tools and inspired by transformative principles, and ready to take on the leading role in creating your reality.

I invite you to continue dancing with conscious projection, with joy, enthusiasm, faith, trust, gratitude, and an open mind and heart to all the infinite possibilities that the universe has to offer you. May your dance be increasingly fluid, harmonious, creative, abundant, joyful, meaningful, and full of love. May your journey of conscious co-creation be an extraordinary adventure, a transformative experience and a richly lived life, in all moments and in all directions.

With deep gratitude for your company on this journey, with joy to witness your awakening as a conscious co-creator, and with enthusiasm for the new horizons that open up before you, I say goodbye, for now, wishing you a continuous, abundant dance, joyful and infinitely creative on the journey of co-creating your conscious reality!

With love and wishes for a continuous and prosperous dance.

www.ingramcontent.com/pod-product-compliance
Lightning Source LLC
LaVergne TN
LVHW040048080526
838202LV00045B/3544